For Elaine Jenks Emerson, dear friend of my
dear Cammy, with best life
that will near perfec....

— Charlie Bryan
11/1/2015

D0847907

Imperfect Past:

History in a New Light

ESSAYS BY

Charles F. Bryan, Jr., Ph.D.

DEMENTI
MILESTONE PUBLISHING

First Printing

Copyright © 2015 by Charles F. Bryan, Jr.

All rights reserved. No part of this book may be reproduced or transmitted in any form or by any means, electronically or mechanically, including photocopying, recording, or by any information storage and retrieval system, without written permission.

Publisher and Design
Wayne Dementi
Dementi Milestone Publishing, Inc.
Manakin-Sabot, VA 23103

www.dementimilestonepublishing.com

The Library of Congress Control Number: 2015933962

ISBN: 978-0-9909613-4-5

Cover design: Sarah Lapallo, Inkwell Book Company

Page Layout: Dianne Dementi

Printed in the United States

A full good faith effort has been made to trace copyright holders and to obtain their permission for the use of copyright material. The publisher apologizes for any omissions or errors and would appreciate notification of any corrections that should be incorporated in future reprints or editions of this book.

DEDICATION

To Cammy, the love of my life, and our legacy —
Alethea, Glenn, Graham, Jackson, Charles, Angela, and
Olivia — all of whom have made our past and future
perfect.

PRAISE
for
𝕴mperfect 𝕻ast: *History in a New Light*

"Bravo, Charlie Bryan! This collection of essays was a delight to read. Few historians have done as much to bring American history to life for so many people and in so many ways as he has."

> – David McCullough
> Pulitzer Prize winning historian

Charles Bryan has a true genius for reaching a very large public with history of the utmost seriousness. It is a rare gift, and he has put it to work with high success. With his leadership, the Virginia Historical Society became the most expansive, the most creative, and the most prosperous institution of its kind. Its inventive historical programs attracted people young and old on a scale I have never seen, and with an intensity of engagement that is unique in my experience. And always Charles Bryan does it with honor, integrity, and a gentleman's grace. He has had the same success in many roles, and we have much to learn from him. The title of his new book, 𝕴mperfect 𝕻ast: *History in a New Light,* is a perfect description of his approach. Its essays are a learning experience of enduring value for anyone who has the pleasure of reading them. His daughter's beautifully written and stunningly poignant essay on the tragedy at Sandy Hook School is an added bonus for the readers of this volume.

> – David Hackett Fischer
> Twice winner of the Pulitzer
> Prize in history, and author
> of *Washington's Crossing* and
> *Paul Revere's Ride.*

Few historians write about the past and how it reaches into today's lives with greater insight than Charles F. Bryan, Jr. His meditations are personal, accessible, occasionally provocative, and always compelling.

> – Rick Atkinson
> Pulitzer Prize winning author
> of six books, including *The Liberation Trilogy,* a comprehensive history of the American Army in Europe in World War II

"I have been a regular reader of the *Richmond Times-Dispatch* for most of my adult life. I have not always agreed with the editorial policies, but have appreciated that I was always allowed the opportunity to express that in writing which was for the most part published. I must say, however, that I always look forward to reading Charles Bryan's essays. I learn something from them almost every time because of the interesting perspectives he brings to his subjects. He deals with factual rather than revisionist reflection. Although I have read most of his essays over the years, I look forward to learning from them again all in one volume."

> – The Honorable L. Douglas Wilder
> former Governor of Virginia and Mayor of Richmond

Charles Bryan led the Virginia Historical Society for two decades, and along the way, became one of the most successful and influential public historians in the United States. Holder of the Ph.D. and the Distinguished Alumnus Award for 2015 from the University of Tennessee history department, Bryan had little time for the intensive research necessary for academic monographs, but he practiced historical interpretation with his editorial essays for the *Richmond Times-Dispatch.* His bold and sometimes contrarian arguments, now collected in *Imperfect Past: History in a New Light,* exhibit over and again the value of Clio's art in the hands of a master.

–   Robert J. Norrell
    author of *Up From History: The Life of Booker T. Washington* and *Alex Haley and the Books that Changed America* (forthcoming)

ACKNOWLEDGEMENTS

𝕴𝖒𝖕𝖊𝖗𝖋𝖊𝖈𝖙 𝕻𝖆𝖘𝖙: *History in a New Light* benefitted from the generosity, advice, and assistance of many people. Several individuals at the Richmond *Times-Dispatch* made it possible to publish this book. Two in particular stand out for their support. Publisher and President Tom Silvestri not only gave me permission to publish the essays I have written for the paper over the years, he wrote a preface for this book that made me blush at first reading. I thank him for his support of this project from its beginning.

I give special acknowledgement to my editor, fellow Baltimore Orioles fan, and friend, Bob Rayner, Commentary Editor and Columnist for the *Times-Dispatch*. For the last five years, Bob has patiently read and edited all of my commentary submissions to the paper. He has never failed to give them good placement in the Sunday edition, and his subtle edits have always improved my essays. For this project, he spent hours tracking down digital copies of some seventy-five of my commentary pieces in the archives of the *Times-Dispatch*. His Archives Manager, Heather Moon, has been indispensable. This book would not have been possible without Bob's help.

Wayne Dementi, President of Dementi Milestone Publishing, has been an essential partner in the production of 𝕴𝖒𝖕𝖊𝖗𝖋𝖊𝖈𝖙 𝕻𝖆𝖘𝖙. I had known Wayne for years, first as a fellow Rotarian, but over the last decade as the publisher of high quality books. When I decided to publish my essays, I went to Wayne. His enthusiastic response to my idea and his obvious knowledge of the publishing business impressed me, and I have not regretted my decision to go with Dementi Milestone Publishing. Wayne has gently prodded me, keeping me on task to meet deadlines he set. He has offered numerous suggestions that have improved the look and quality of this book. I could not have asked for a better publisher.

Another key player in this project includes Sandie Warwick, an editor of the first order, who patiently read every one of these essays and made good suggestions and changes throughout. Her keen editorial eye has helped make this a better book.

A good index is an essential part of any nonfiction work. Wayne Dementi picked the ideal person for this task, and I thank Chris Dunn for the excellent one she prepared for this book.

My friend, Allen Mead Ferguson, a gifted writer, prepared the book description for the dust jacket for which I am grateful.

My former colleague at the Virginia Historical Society, Frances Pollard, and her staff have helped me any number of times by tracking down information that is often arcane and obscure. For example, how many movie theaters were in Richmond in 1915? Or when did Virginia's population become more urban than rural. They confirmed their reputation as one of the best library research teams in the country. Thank you, Frances!

A man of many talents, my brother-in-law, Dr. Battle Haslam, took the remarkable photograph of my grandfather and his friend, Roy Webb, in 1962 that appears on page 73. Battle has been like the brother I never had and a special friend for more than fifty years.

My greatest debt is to my wife and best friend, Cammy. She has always been the first person to read my essays, saving me from embarrassment more times than I am willing to admit by pointing out inconsistencies in my text, missing words, and confusing verbage. Little did I know when we married nearly a half century ago that my life partner would play such a key role in improving my writing.

Finally, I want to thank the thousands of readers of my columns in the *Times-Dispatch*, many of whom have encouraged me to publish my writings in one volume. I hope they will enjoy revisiting my commentaries, and I welcome many new readers to my slant on history. To all of them, I hope they will better understand the past by looking at it in a different light.

CONTENTS

FOREWORD

By

Tom Silvestri

Just before Christmas 2014, Charlie Bryan paid one of his regular visits to the *Richmond Times-Dispatch*. He is no stranger. During his days leading the Virginia Historical Society, Charlie often popped up in news stories and features. Richmond, after all, loves history. Reporters relish insightful news sources. So, Charlie was the nexus, with his crisp quotes and insightful observations hitting home.

After his retirement, he became a frequent contributor to our Sunday Commentary section, a reader favorite because it is a weekly, high-quality collaboration of viewpoints that examine international, national, state, regional and local issues. We are unusual among regional newspapers our size in the large number of opinion pieces we publish from informed members of the community who also are good writers. We think that's a positive reflection on Richmond and the majority's preference for a robust but civil dialogue about civic issues of importance to Richmond and to the commonwealth of Virginia.

On that score, Charlie is probably our best contributor who isn't a part of the *Times-Dispatch* staff. Over the years, he and Commentary Editor Bob Rayner made a habit of turning a jewel of a story into a dominant section-front centerpiece, complete with attractive illustrations from one of our staff artists. But based on the volume of his outstanding essays, you could make the point he's as much a part of the *Times-Dispatch* family as the editor, the chief political columnist, the controller and even the publisher. And we think that's just

Tom Silvestri

peachy-keen -- a hyphenated word that you might find unexpectedly in a Charlie essay because he likes to deliver pleasant surprises.

When he arranged a check-in meeting with Bob, I was happy to join him at the *Times-Dispatch's* downtown Richmond headquarters. Once you see a scheduled discussion with Charlie on the calendar, it's something to look forward to -- a break in the action that's guaranteed to stimulate the brain with knowledge and pepper it with a little historic intrigue from his latest essay. This time, Charlie had a request.

He wanted to know if we would grant him permission to publish a book of his commentaries that appeared in the capital-region newspaper since 1992. He was excited that his passion for storytelling had achieved a substantial collection of essays that covered many diverse topics and were now at such a high total that they could fill a book of 200 pages.

A book? we asked.

Yes, please, he said.

Wow, have we published that many, Charlie? we responded.

He smiled.

Yes, indeed.

Putting out a daily newspaper tends to blur the significance of an individual's accomplishment. It is unintentional. We just expect interesting stories, thought-provoking columns, and breaking news to be there day after day after day. Controversies come and go. News is even more perishable these days. Digital products have sped up the pace. The newspaper and now its website are a rapidly rolling account of raw history that never stops. Rarely is there time to pause on what we've done in the past, besides the almost clichéd year-in-review compendium.

Frankly, we consider each day's edition to be a book in itself. At the *Times-Dispatch*, an editor once had a Sunday newspaper converted into a paperbook form to make that exact point. When the result arrived, she had a three-inch volume along the lines of *War and Peace*. That's not a bold revelation since those world realities were probably covered in the book-size pages anyway.

Charlie's intent to convert his series of essays into a book stopped us for a moment. Should the *Times-Dispatch* be the publisher? We quickly answered no. Well, in a sense, we are the original publisher but Charlie already had another one lined up just in case. And we are familiar with the good work of the Dementi Milestone Press, a local business that's made respectful use of *Times-Dispatch* photographs in its other books.

Frankly, given the long list of projects we had already, we told Charlie to go the independent route. The last thing we wanted to happen was the *Times-Dispatch* delaying or unnecessarily slowing Charlie's book desire. "You have a green light here," I said to him.

Then came the second ask. Can you help me locate all of the columns in the RTD? Charlie requested. That task fell to Bob, the keeper of Commentary content. Over the next several weeks, Bob would retrieve blocks of the published pieces as he shared them with Charlie. He'd package them up in bunches, according to the year they appeared. Bob also made a habit of sending them to me via email after Charlie used a third ask for an introduction to the book.

This is a first for me. It's also an honor to be associated with his collection. When Charlie sent me the quotes from three Pulitzer Prize-winning historians and authors, I said only Charlie could assemble four Pulitzer writers to deliver endorsing accolades. David McCullough (one of my favorite biographers), David Hackett Fischer (I have many of his books about the American Revolution), Rick Atkinson (his World War II work is stunning) and Tom Silvestri. Except in my case, the prize would be for best memo about a business problem or solution. Just for the record, no such category exists. (The Pulitzer people need to do something about that.)

Bob's routine of finding and then sending Charlie's essays -- "nonfiction," as he likes to remind everyone -- became a welcome break from the monotony of daily business communication. The commentaries on each email were nestled among industry newsletters, pitches for business services, reader complaints, compliments or questions, and requests for approvals related to *Times-Dispatch* proposals.

Charlie's writings were pleasant interludes. Like catching up with a trusted friend. As you would expect with an historian who headed a Virginia history museum, there's a healthy concentration on the Civil War. Charlie used a good chunk of his time with *Times-Dispatch* readers to offer a slightly different angle to the known arguments. He also didn't shy away from conclusions that could spark further debate and displeasure.

In the May 2012 essay "The Danger Of Denying A Hard History," you sense the many head-banging discussions Charlie had with those devoted to certain causes. He masterfully mixes observations from a trip to Europe with thoughts about "my native South and its most wrenching experience." He applauds the four-year Civil War sesquicentennial commemorations for embracing "the full story of probably the most tragic period in our nation's history, a far cry from the almost celebratory atmosphere of the war's centennial 50 years ago." His last sentence is a quote worthy of chiseling in the granite wall of an open-minded historic attraction: "To ignore the unpleasant realities of the past is the ultimate form of denial."

In reading the essays again, a mainstay remains his assessments of what the War of Northern Aggression was really about. But you'd also find a refreshing dose of the offbeat that delves into sports, food, the weather and travel.

Consider these headlines that introduced Charlie's essays:

"Books That Change History" (published April 2010).

"Until Recently, Winter Was A Most Dangerous Season" (April 2013).

"America's Cathedrals of Democracy" (October 2010)

"The Civil War Transformed American Medicine" (July 2013)

"Americans Rely On Their (News)Papers for 300 Years" (October 2012). In it, Charlie wrote this paragraph that captured my industry better than some journalists writing about newspapers: "Many experts argue that a new business model is needed in the U.S. Others contend that the print media are not dying but simply evolving into a new form. Whether it is delivered on paper or electronically, uncensored, up-to-date and informative news will continue to be a bedrock of the American democratic experience." Can I get an Amen on that score?

"Why Do Americans Give" July 2012

"Armed Forces Integrated 60 Years Ago" (July 2008)

"Gettysburg's Dark Secret" (June 2013)

"Even Without Braves, Boulevard Blessed," showing his side interest (March 2008) in baseball and his worry about museums not getting the financial support they're due. "What if our area museums ceased operations or left Richmond like the Braves?"

"The Making Of A Superior Wartime Leader (March 2011)

"A Delicious History of Southern Food" (November 2012)

"Ten Places All Americans Should Visit" (June 2010), a list that had these qualifications: "It is on American soil; it has historic significance; it is a widely recognized icon; or it is closely tied to our national identity." By the way, Virginia showed up as No. 8 with The Historic Quadrangle. "Individually, Jamestown, Williamsburg and Richmond played crucial roles in American history. But within this relatively small area are the sites of the first permanent English settlement and representative self-government in America, an incubator of American independence, the last major engagement of the Revolution, the national capital of the war for Southern independence, and numerous Civil War battles." Classic Charlie context.

"Deadlier Than War; The Great Flu Pandemic" (January 2013)

"The Man Who Taught America To Read" (March 2013)

And finally, there's Charlie's first column, "Take A Stroll Through Virginia's Rich History," published on Nov. 23, 1992. Page A-7. It was about the recent expansion of the Virginia Historical Society and its priority to create a "Museum of Virginia History" as the most comprehensive interpretation of Virginia's past to be found in the Commonwealth.

"Without question," he wrote, "the Old Dominion has a history that few states can match and some of the finest history museums in the country. From Colonial Williamsburg to Monticello to the Valentine Museum, specific aspects and periods of Virginia history are interpreted very effectively. This approach to learning the full scope of Virginia's past, however, tends to be episodic and scattered. We must travel to several museums to learn about colonial history, to historic houses to put important families and early leaders into any meaningful context, to many battlefields and the Museum of the Confederacy to understand the ebb and flow of events of the Civil War, or to a host of local museums to learn about a particular community's past. Except for a few local museums, history after Appomattox too often overlooked entirely."

During his two decades at the helm of the Virginia Historical Society, Charlie Bryan worked to change that picture. It is a powerful canvas that continues to expand in colorful strokes with his successor and the museum's resilient staff.

In retirement, Charlie continues to write. "His columns are immensely popular among our readers because he combines a natural storyteller's eye for the telling detail with a professional historian's grasp of the deeper meaning and broad consequences of the people and events he chronicles," Bob Rayner told me when I asked him why we publish Charlie's essays. "He never avoids drawing sharp, sometimes painful conclusions about our past, but his work is always tempered by compassion and good humor."

The *Richmond Times-Dispatch* is fortunate to be publisher of Charlie Bryan's interpretations about Virginia history. We cheer the reappearance of his excellent work in this book and applaud you, the reader, for finding the time to enjoy the stories written by a first-rate historian who always will remain one of us.

We don't mind saying this: Charlie, you do us proud.

*****

*Tom Silvestri has been the president and publisher of the **Richmond Times-Dispatch** since January 2005 and a resident of the Richmond Region since 1982. He had nothing to do with his birth in Yonkers, NY. He considers himself a Virginian.*

⊸o⊶

INTRODUCTION

Learning to Write

by

Charles F. Bryan, Jr.

Two high school classes proved invaluable in shaping my future as a writer—basic typing and creative writing.

I took typing as an elective mainly because I had a crush on the most beautiful girl in my school. Fortunately she paid little attention to me. As a result I wasn't distracted, and I became a decent typist, something that has served me well as a writer to this day.

Even more significant in my education was a class taught by Mrs. Jean Myers. She was a little wisp of a woman, who like most good teachers, was demanding and impatient if she thought you were not reaching your full potential. She was a math teacher, and I never did well in those classes of hers. I felt lucky to earn a C+ in her honors algebra class.

Fortunately, she also taught creative writing. As our text, she chose *The Elements of Style* by William Strunk and E.B. White. My well-worn copy is still a beloved member of my personal library. *Elements* has been described as "a forty-three page summation of the case for cleanliness, accuracy, and brevity in the use of English." Strunk and White laid out eighteen rules such as "omit needless words" and "use the active voice" that have guided me ever since.

Recently we cleaned out our attic, and I found a box of my old class notes and term papers, a few from high school, but most from my college days at the Virginia Military Institute. Included in this personal archive was a short essay I wrote for freshman English titled "A Dream of the Past." In it I compared my carefree life in high school to what I was experiencing at VMI, where my world was "a blur of gray, brightened here and there by the flash of a friend's wit, a letter from home, or weekend free from confinement and marching penalty tours."

My professor, the legendary Colonel Herbert Nash Dillard, awarded me an "A" for the paper, commenting that "now, when you get into the world, you'll say the same damned thing about VMI." Thanks to Jean Myers's teaching, my "A" was the only one awarded in the class, but it was also one of the few "A's" I earned in college.

Indeed, my academic record at VMI was not distinguished. I ended my first year on academic probation, and I eventually graduated with a paltry 2.1 grade point average. Even though I majored in history, VMI required its liberal arts majors to take subjects that were more like an obstacle course on the way to graduation. Low grades in algebra, trigonometry, chemistry, and economics pulled my final average down to such an extent that I worried that I would not graduate with my class.

I was fortunate to be able to get into graduate school, but once there and with history as my area of concentration, I thrived as a student for the first time in my life. My ability to write well, learned in high school and at VMI, worked to my advantage.

French historian Marc Bloch argued that the key to being a good historian is an ability to ask the right questions. Just as important is the ability to answer them effectively with the written and spoken word. Soon after graduating from VMI, I married Cammy Martin, whom I dated for three years and would become my best friend and editor for the next half century.

After a two-year hitch in the Army, I eventually earned my Ph.D. in history from the University of Tennessee, where my major professor, Paul Bergoron, honed my writing skills. I thought then that becoming a historian meant that I would be a college professor and scholar. I assumed that my insights into history would be passed on to students in the classroom and to my fellow historians through my scholarly writing.

It never worked out that way, and in retrospect I am grateful. When I completed my Ph.D. in the late 1970's, the odds of landing a college teaching job, especially in the field of American history, were slim. In the three decades after World War II, universities turned out far more Ph.D. graduates in the liberal arts, including history, than the job market could absorb. By the time I earned my doctorate, it was not unusual to see a hundred applications for a single teaching job.

I was turned down for every teaching position I pursued. My fellow graduate students and I were envious when one in our group landed a job at a community college in Eastern Kentucky. I became deeply discouraged, and even contemplated giving up my dream of becoming a historian.

Then, I was fortunate to be awarded a one-year post-doctoral fellowship from the National Archives in historical documentary editing at The Hermitage, the home of Andrew Jackson, near Nashville. The internship, involving editing the personal and official papers of America's seventh president, evolved into an appointment as assistant editor of the project. Nevertheless, I saw this opportunity as a temporary stopgap until I could land a full-time teaching job. In the meantime, I taught the American history survey course in the evening at the local community college.

Three and a half years later, I found myself working in history outside of the classroom when I landed my first job as the executive director of a historical organization, the East Tennessee Historical Society. The five years I spent there proved invaluable in helping shape my future career. I had to do **everything**: mount exhibitions, write and edit publications, develop and lead educational programs, work with a board, supervise staff and volunteers, write grant proposals, work with collections, and oversee membership programs.

I had become a "public historian" rather than the traditional academic historian. My work allowed me to bring history directly to the general public, and I loved it. Subsequent directorships at the St. Louis Mercantile Library and especially the twenty years I spent as president of the Virginia Historical Society gave me the opportunity to work in the field of history in ways that I never dreamed.

But the higher I moved up the ladder of the public history profession, the less I was able to "do history," to actually research and write on my own. Most of my time was consumed with introducing new programs, fundraising, overseeing building projects, supervising staff, frequent speaking to the general public, working with board members, and strategic planning.

I wrote occasional articles for professional museum journals, book reviews for scholarly journals, and early in my career, I published half a dozen articles for *Civil War Times Illustrated*. Upon reaching my tenth anniversary at the Virginia Historical Society, the board of trustees granted me a three month sabbatical to work on a book with Nelson Lankford that became a Civil War bestseller, *Eye of the Storm: A Civil War Odyssey*, published in 2000 by the Free Press, a division of Simon and Schuster.

A few years after *Eye of the Storm* was published, I began writing occasional pieces for the commentary section of the *Richmond Times-Dispatch*. The RTD has long accepted guest commentary articles on a variety of issues. These early columns of mine usually related to my work at the Virginia Historical Society such as fundraising and exhibitions we were mounting.

I was diagnosed with Parkinson's disease in 2004, and ironically the urge to write grew stronger in me. I realized that this debilitating disease would eventually prevent me from doing not only the routine aspects of life that we take for granted such as dressing myself, driving, and keyboarding (what we used to call typing). But it would also keep me from traveling abroad, outdoor physical activities, and possibly from being able to write.

I decided to retire early at age 62 from the Virginia Historical Society in large part to do those things that I shouldn't put off too far into an uncertain future. At the same time, I did not want to break completely from being a public historian and from writing. To remain involved in public history, I contacted my good friend Dan Jordan, the soon to retire president of the Thomas Jefferson Foundation, which owns Monticello, to see if he would be interested forming a consulting firm specializing in helping nonprofit institutions, especially those that are history-related. He agreed, and our business venture, Bryan & Jordan Consulting, has turned out to be far more successful than we ever anticipated, so much so that time for writing became harder to come by than I thought it would.

I also found myself writing for the *Times-Dispatch*, now mostly on history. Composing them with a limit of 750 words was a challenging but fun exercise in writing. I enjoyed writing the columns so much that I proposed to Bob Rayner, associate editor of the RTD editorial page, that I would be willing to write a monthly commentary piece without compensation. Fortunately, the RTD agreed to my proposal

Beginning in early 2011, I started writing pieces every few weeks on a variety of topics, but mostly history. I also decided that my columns would not be limited to a particular field of history. Having taught the American history survey course on the college level early in my career helped give me a large mental warehouse of potential subjects to write. That classroom experience also helped me determine my readership.

I would write my essays with the general public in mind, people who had some knowledge of history, but were not experts. Each essay would be similar to a presentation I would have given when I taught the freshman survey history course. And much as I did when I taught, I would attempt to bring new perspectives to certain topics, and to let my readers see history in a different light.

In recent years, a number of commentators have complained that the writing and teaching of American history has put too much emphasis on its negative aspects. That it has over emphasized critical thinking. One prominent radio talk show host argues that students should not have their minds muddled by differing interpretations of history. To him: "History is real simple. You know what it is? It's what happened." He apparently does not recognize that views of the past can change with time and as new evidence is found.

I think that critics like him are perhaps unhappy that a once seemingly simple and comforting story of America's past has become more complex, more unsettling, more provocative, and, I would add, more compelling. People in the past were not perfect. Events of yesteryear were no less controversial than they are today.

A few of my columns did not fit into the category of history, but rather were ruminations by me on contemporary issues or personal matters such as my battle with Parkinson's disease, problems relating to homeless veterans, and the world-wide dissemination of southern cuisine. But even those columns draw on the past to provide perspective.

Since submitting my first column to the RTD, I have written nearly eighty in all. People often ask me how I decide on topics. The reasons vary. Occasionally I tie them to anniversaries such as the sesquicentennial of the Civil War or the centennial of World War I. Sometimes they come from suggestions by readers, such as my column on world-renowned sculptor, Sir Moses Ezekiel, an idea that came from Sam Witt, whose business office is near mine. Quite often ideas have popped in my head when I'm on a walk or driving. Current events sometimes inspire me to write.

Once I decide on a topic, I try to read as much as I can from secondary sources, especially the most up-to-date scholarship. Yes, Google, Wikipedia, and any number of other online sources have proven invaluable in providing the information I need to write about a subject.

I write my pieces without an outline or any preconceived notions of how they will unfold or end. I attribute that to telling stories to my daughter, son, and their friends when they were children. I now regale their children with similar tales. My stories usually revolve around Jeff and Elmo, two fictional early teenage boys who have enough adventures to last anyone a lifetime, including getting lost in a coalmine, rescuing survivors of a downed airplane, and finding a chest full of gold on an island.

Great writers of history—David McCullough, Bruce Catton, Barbara Tuchman, David Hackett Fischer, Doris Kearns Goodwin, Rick Atkinson—are also great storytellers. I am neither a great writer nor a great storyteller, but I try to tell a compelling narrative in what I write.

When my columns became a regular feature of the RTD, people began asking me if I had ever thought about republishing them in one volume. At first, I dismissed the suggestion, but I began to hear it enough that I finally decided to do just that.

The *Richmond Times-Dispatch* graciously gave me permission to reprint as many of the articles as I wished. Three were not published in the paper, but one that was is not even mine. Instead it is a remarkable essay by my daughter, Alethea Bryan Gerding, soon after the tragic massacre at Sandy Hook School in 2012. As soon as she sent it to me and I read it, I forwarded it to the editorial staff of the *Times-Dispatch*, who were as moved as I was by her words. I consider her essay the best in this volume, and I only wish she would use her special gift as a writer more than she is able to.

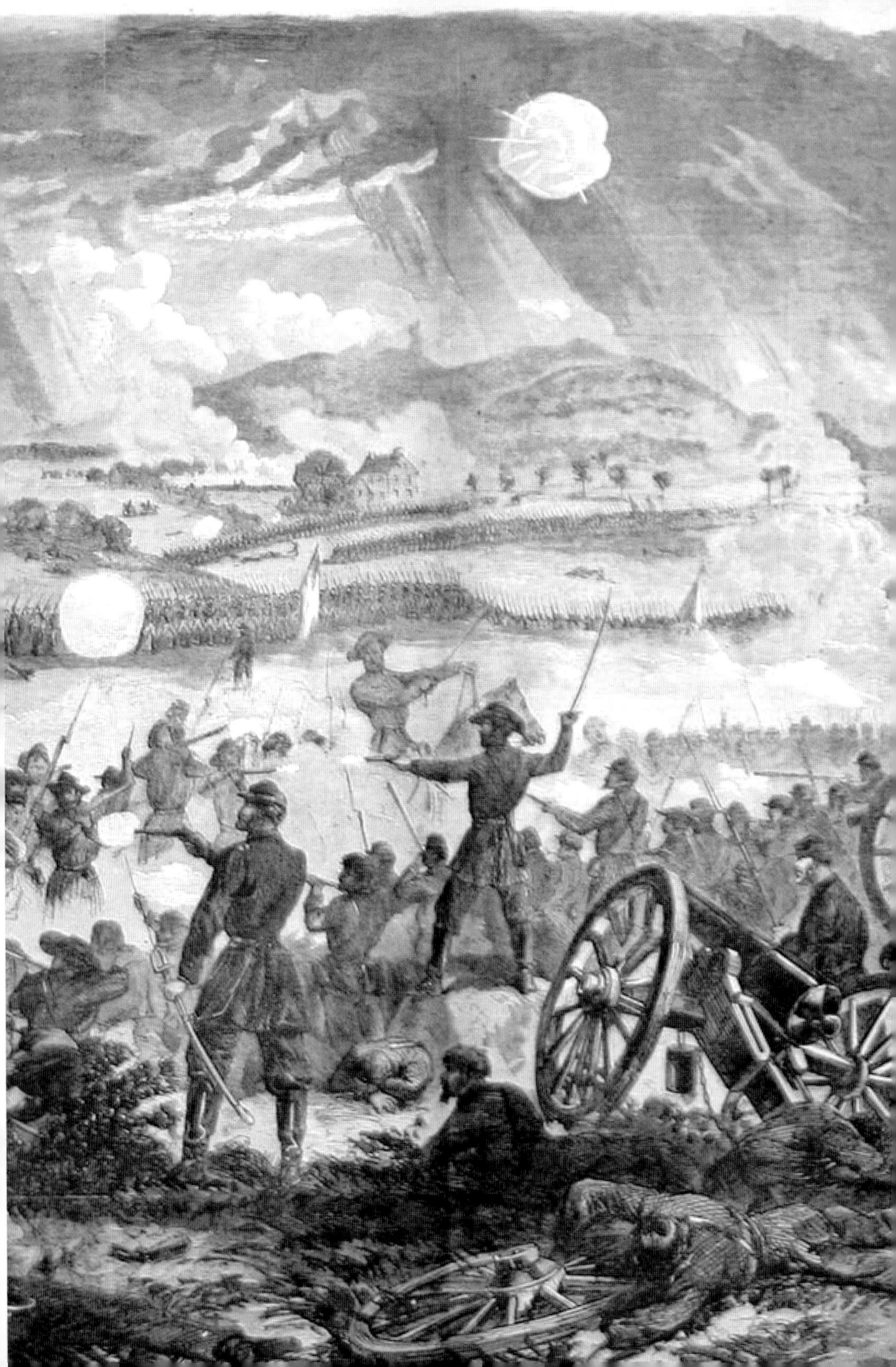

PART I

THE CIVIL WAR: AMERICA UNHINGED

The Civil War is the most studied subject in American history. More than 50,000 books have been published on that cataclysmic event; and even though it slips farther into the past with each succeeding year, interest never seems to wane. It is the story of Cain and Abel writ large. Indeed, it contains all of the elements of great storytelling—heroes and villains, triumph and tragedy, winners and losers, death and destruction, the enslaved and the free.

I developed a profound interest in the Civil War in my youth, fueled by vivid stories told to me by my elders. It was a fascination that continued to grow and eventually led me to earn a Ph.D. in history with a specialty in the period. It is little wonder that I have written more essays on this subject than any other.

Also, during the last four years, our country marked the 150th anniversary of the Civil War. It seemed only fitting that I share some insights into that monumental conflict, providing readers with a few perspectives that might help them see the war in a different light.

1

Yes, Slavery Caused the Civil War

Abraham Lincoln was elected president of the United States 150 years ago. Within six months of the election, eleven Southern states seceded from the Union to form the Confederate States of America. Soon North and South were plunged into a ghastly civil war that resulted in losses proportionally comparable to the European nations during the world wars.

What caused such a national calamity? Why did Southerners react so radically to a presidential election? Those questions have been raised from the moment the guns went silent the spring of 1865. With the Civil War sesquicentennial commemoration fast approaching us, the debate has begun anew.

A range of theories have been advanced to find the answers, including states' rights, divergent regional economies, different cultural identities, variations in demographic makeup, leadership failures on the national and state levels, and slavery.

Each of those factors has a valid place in explaining the war's origins, but one has been the most hotly debated and persistent - slavery. Because most Southerners did not own slaves, slavery could not have been the issue, argues one side. Furthermore, most Northerners were not particularly opposed to the institution.

Contrary views posit that the percentage of slave ownership is irrelevant. Human bondage was the underpinning of the Southern economy and a primary means of social control over the region's black population. To do away with the institution threatened the economic and social fabric of the South. And while Northerners may not have been against slavery per se, they were opposed to its spread into the Western territory, while Southerners maintained the opposite view.

Which argument is the stronger?

Scholars have long studied Southern secession. The consensus now is that slavery was the primary cause. Without slavery, historians argue, there would have been no need for the South to secede and create a new nation.

What is their evidence? One has only to look at the minutes of the individual state secession conventions and the words of the Confederate States of America constitution to find the answers.

In 1860-61, each of the eleven states making up the Confederacy met in separate conventions to debate secession and to decide their future. The election of Lincoln and the defense of slavery dominated their deliberations. Rabid secessionists skillfully portrayed Lincoln as an abolitionist and a certain threat to the institution. A North Carolinian asserted that Lincoln intended to end slavery and give the newly freed blacks "all the privileges of white men."

When South Carolina became the first state to leave the Union, it issued pleas to the other Southern states "to join us in forming a Confederacy of slaveholding states." The Virginia secession convention adopted resolutions asserting the preservation of slavery and full recognition of slavery in the territories. A commissioner to the Texas secession convention proclaimed "the people of the slaveholding States are bound together by the same necessity and determination to preserve African slavery."

Many Southerners who opposed secession ironically invoked slavery in their arguments by prophetically asserting that the institution actually would be better protected in the Union than in a Confederacy that was sure to fail. Southern Unionists in Appalachia railed against the new Southern republic, vowing to never be "hewers of wood for the slave aristocracy.

The Confederate constitution is almost a carbon copy of the United States Constitution, with a handful of exceptions, the most important being slavery. While the federal constitution remains silent on slavery other than barring foreign importation of people in bondage, its Confederate counterpart contains four clauses asserting slavery's legality and guaranteeing against any law that would threaten the institution. As Confederate Vice President Alexander Stephens asserted after the constitution was adopted: "Our new government is founded upon. . . the great truth that slavery. . . is [the Negro's] natural and normal state."

Some people still claim that the Civil War was not about slavery. Solid documentary evidence, however, undermines their arguments. The Confederacy was a nation based on laws and constitutional authority protecting slavery and the right of its citizens to own other human beings.

Had North and South not disagreed over slavery, Southerners would not have felt threatened by the election of Lincoln, a perceived abolitionist president. It was something they were willing to fight and die for.

Richmond Times Dispatch, August 15, 2010

2

FLOCKING TO THE COLORS: THE NAIVE RUSH TO JOIN UP

Since ancient times, young men have flocked to the colors and taken up arms in the early stages of a war. Inevitably, however, the initial rush to the ranks peters out as grim reports of death and maiming reach home. Our Civil War was no exception.

Seldom in American history have men been as eager to fight as they were 150 years ago. Soon after Confederate forces fired on Fort Sumter and President Lincoln's call for 75,000 volunteers to put down the Southern rebellion, the nation plunged into civil war.

Southerners stormed recruiting stations, eager to risk their lives in defense of their homeland, while Northerners rallied in huge numbers to join the army and save the Union. "So impatient did I become for starting," recalled one recruit, "that I felt like ten thousand pins were pricking me in every part of my body."

Little by little, recruits were formed into regiments and learned to drill. The young soldiers were full of hope, waving flags made by their sweethearts, and anxious to engage the enemy. Almost everyone expected a short war, prompting many recruits to fear missing their chance for glory on the battlefield.

Yet within a year, the Confederacy was forced to institute a draft. The North followed suit in 1863.

Threatened by expiring term enlistments and after sustaining staggering battlefield losses and deaths to disease, the respective armies faced severe manpower shortages. Both Presidents Davis and Lincoln regarded conscription as the only means of sustaining a sufficient army.

From the beginning, compulsory service embittered the public, North and South.

Many people considered conscription an infringement on individual freedom and personal liberty. Arguing with some justification that reluctant soldiers made poor fighting men, volunteer soldiers never regarded draftees as their equals. They complained that it hurt morale and compromised unit cohesion.

The most controversial aspect of Civil War conscription was its exemptions. Both Confederate and Union draft laws allowed propertied men, particularly Southern slaveholders, to avoid military service, leaving the burden on men with limited resources.

Northerners with the wherewithal could pay a substitute to take their place in the army. Unfair, unpopular and poorly conceived, the respective draft systems raised more public resentment than soldiers. Ironically the draft laws actually stimulated volunteer recruiting.

Conscription was not enough, however, to fill the ranks as the war dragged on. New recruiting measures were required, including targeting newly arrived immigrants in the North for service.

Also by mid-war the Union launched a bold and controversial initiative -- the enlistment of black troops. Almost overwhelmed by vast numbers of refugee slaves behind Union lines, Federal authorities began to recognize the immense reserve of manpower represented by newly freed slaves.

In 1863 the government authorized Negro regiments. Although initially relegated to manual labor, by 1864 black troops were committed to combat. The Union put some 150,000 black men into uniform, representing ten percent of all federal troops during the war. They played a vital role in helping secure Union victory.

By early 1865, even the Confederacy began to contemplate arming slaves to fill their depleted ranks. "We must decide," noted Robert E. Lee, "whether the negroes shall fight for us or against us."

The proposal initially met furious protests, but in March a desperate Confederate Congress passed legislation authorizing the mustering of 300,000 black soldiers. By then, it was too late. In less than a month, the Confederacy collapsed.

We have seen vestiges of the Civil War recruiting saga in recent years. In the immediate aftermath of the 9/11 terrorist attacks on America, a surge of young people signed on to the armed forces. Yet within a few years, as casualties mounted in Iraq and Afghanistan, and military units experienced multiple deployments, recruiting slipped badly. Standards were lowered to meet quotas and, similar to Civil War days, the services began to rely more heavily on recent immigrants to fill their ranks. Since then, however, recruiting has rebounded, which many experts attribute largely to high unemployment and a significant reduction in combat casualties.

Years after the Civil War, Union Gen. William T. Sherman admonished a crowd of youths saying, "There is many a boy here today who looks on war as all glory, but, boys, it is all hell. You can bear this warning voice to generations yet to come."

Unfortunately future generations would march off to seeming glory only to learn firsthand that war is, indeed, hell.

Richmond Times Dispatch, August 7, 2011

3

GENERALS LEE AND THOMAS MADE HARD CHOICES: CIVIL WAR SPLIT

L ife is full of decisions. When you are a child, most decisions are made for you, but as you grow older and mature, you decide more for yourself. Decisions become more complex and harder to make because they often are life-altering choices that can lead to success or ruin.

Then there are decisions that force you to choose the "harder right," a concept drilled into every cadet at the United States Military Academy at West Point. It teaches that often the right decisions in life are the hardest decisions to make. It starts with the West Point honor code, which simply states that a cadet "will not lie, cheat, or steal, nor tolerate those who do." In other words, if you see a friend cheating or lying, you are obliged to report him for an honor violation. Later as an officer in the army, it may mean putting yourself at risk for the good of your unit. In one way or another, everyone has had to make harder right decisions in life. But few of us have made the harder right decisions that two Virginians were forced to make. Their names were Robert E. Lee and George H. Thomas. In many ways they were alike. Both had deep roots in their native land, dating to the seventeenth century when their English ancestors came to Virginia. They were born only ninety miles apart into slaveholding families. Both had difficult childhoods, losing their fathers when they were boys.

Both Entered West Point

Because their families were strapped financially, both young men chose a path to a college education that was free and offered attractive career opportunities. Lee graduated second in the class of 1829 without a demerit. Thomas finished the Academy in 1840 in the top ranks of his class. Both men married and began successful military careers. Lee became an army engineer. Thomas served in the artillery and later in the cavalry.

Both men fought with distinction in the Mexican-American War. They displayed degrees of bravery and leadership that marked them for great things in the future. After the war, Thomas returned on leave to his home in Southampton County to a hero's welcome. Lee came back to his family in Arlington flushed with success. Then for the only time in their lives the two Virginians served together when they were assigned to one of the army's most elite cavalry units stationed on the Indian frontier in Texas.

Lee and Thomas. So remarkably alike—until 1861. After the election of Abraham Lincoln as President, the states of the lower South seceded and formed the new Confederate nation. Then in April, 1861, Southern forces fired on Fort Sumter. Soon after, states from the upper South, including Virginia, joined the Confederacy. Then hundreds of native-born Southerners serving in the United States Army had a momentous choice. Would they remain loyal to the Union or would they go with the South? The majority decided to put on the gray uniform. What about the two Virginians who seemed so much alike?

Lee Chose His Native State

Soon after Fort Sumter, President Lincoln offered Lee command of all Union forces. The Virginian had a harder right decision to make. Would he serve the country he had sworn to defend or would he go with his fellow Virginians? He answered that he would follow his native state "with my sword, and if need be, with my life." After a year of secondary commands and staff jobs, he assumed command of the Confederate army in Virginia in June, 1862. Then for nearly three years he won a remarkable string of victories and led a gallant defense against heavier odds before eventually surrendering to U.S. Grant at Appomattox in 1865. He is regarded as one of the great military commanders in American history.

What about the other Virginian? Soon after Fort Sumter, Virginia Governor John Letcher offered Thomas command of all state artillery forces. Many people throughout Virginia wondered what Thomas would do. Most assumed he would side with the South. Certainly his Virginia family did. But by the end of April, he shocked them by announcing he would remain loyal to the Union. "I took an oath at West Point to defend the Constitution and to serve my country," he declared. "I do not break my oaths."

Like Lee, Thomas proved a great general. He rose steadily in rank, eventually becoming a Union army commander in Tennessee and Georgia. His brilliant defensive stand at the battle of Chickamauga in 1863 earned him the nickname "The Rock of Chickamauga." His forces routed a Confederate army at Chattanooga. He fought effectively with Sherman in the Atlanta campaign. And he destroyed an entire Confederate army at Nashville in the closing months of the war. Historians rank the Virginian as one of the top Union generals of the war.

The war ended in victory for Thomas, but in defeat for Lee. Both men lived another five, often difficult, years, dying within a matter of months of each other. Lee's family fortune and property were lost during the war. For a time, there was talk of his being tried as a traitor. Despite several lucrative job offers, he accepted the presidency of struggling Washington College in Lexington. Within five years he turned the school around, and when he died in 1870, he was one of the most respected and beloved men in the South.

Thomas was not beloved in his native land, but he received the accolades of a grateful nation. At the end of the war, the U.S. Congress passed a resolution in his honor. He was promoted to major general in the regular army and given the command of his choice - the Department of the Pacific, headquartered in San Francisco. But he died suddenly from a massive stroke in 1870. Nearly 10,000 people attended his funeral in New York, far from Virginia, but not a single member of his family showed up. Later someone asked his sisters why they did not attend. "As far as we're concerned, our brother died in 1861," they replied coldly. George Thomas died loyal to the country he swore to defend. But as a result, he severed all ties with his native state and his own flesh and blood.

So who was right - Lee or Thomas? Both had harder right decisions to make. Both suffered for those decisions, losing a lot because of the courage of their convictions. What would you have done if you had been in their shoes? In making your next harder right decision, will you have the same courage of conviction as those two brave Virginia soldiers?

Richmond Times Dispatch, April 11, 2004

4

SEPARATION AND DIVORCE: WEST VIRGINIA VS. VIRGINIA

As we celebrate Independence Day on Monday, it is worth noting that a large portion of Virginia sought its own independence 150 years ago. Like their Patriot forebears, the people of western Virginia advocated separation from the Old Dominion, citing an accumulation of long-held grievances, including unfair taxation and unequal representation.

Just as a troubled marriage has difficulty surviving a catastrophic experience, the fragile relationship between western Virginians and their fellow statesmen would not survive the trauma of civil war. The split sprang from no sudden impulse.

Virginia east of the Alleghenies looked commercially to the seaboard and the South, while the mountainous counties of the west and what is now West Virginia's panhandle gravitated more to the Ohio Valley and northward.

Over time, western Virginians developed numerous complaints against their cousins to the east, who had garnered political power out of proportion to their numbers. With many more slaves in the eastern counties, discrimination in favor of slaveholders in the matters of taxation, limitations on voting and distribution of government benefits built up anger toward the "aristocrats" of the East.

By 1861, a long-simmering resentment in the western counties was ready to explode into open rebellion against authority in Richmond.

After the election of Abraham Lincoln as president, states of the lower South left the Union and formed the Confederate

States of America. Virginia, however, had strong Unionist leanings and initially refused to join the new nation. When Confederate forces fired on Fort Sumter in April, however, and Lincoln called for 75,000 volunteers to suppress the rebellion, the situation changed dramatically.

Four states of the upper South, including Virginia, soon joined the Confederacy. Pro-Union sentiment in Virginia melted away, with one major exception. When Virginia held a popular referendum on secession, its citizens voted overwhelmingly in its favor. Yet more than two-thirds of present-day West Virginia voted against it.

In response, hundreds of Unionists from thirty-eight western Virginia counties convened twice in Wheeling in May 1861 to decide what to do. After considerable debate, the delegates declared the "reorganized government of Virginia." Calling the existing government in Richmond null and void, the Wheeling delegates elected a new set of officials to represent the state, including a governor. They also filled the U.S. Senate and House seats they declared vacated by Confederate Virginians.

Alarmed Confederate and Virginia state authorities condemned these actions, declaring them illegitimate. Confederate forces were rushed in to secure the western counties, and to seize the Federal armory at Harpers Ferry.

For months, Confederate and Union forces struggled for control of the western counties, including a futile campaign by Robert E. Lee. But by early 1862, the Federals had enough troops in the region to prevail for the rest of the war.

Free of Confederate control, western Virginia Unionists sought separate statehood. Meeting in convention, the delegates voted to create a new state named West Virginia. Perhaps most controversial was the absorption of six pro-Confederate counties bordering Virginia that were under Federal occupation. After the ratification of a new constitution in a public referendum in 1862, President Lincoln signed the separate statehood bill as a war measure, and West Virginia was admitted as the thirty-fifth state in the Union in 1863.

The legality of West Virginia statehood has been long debated but never tested in court. Political leaders in Virginia forcefully defended the right of a state to secede from the Union, yet they roundly condemned the actions of the western Virginia counties to secede from the mother state. Unionists argued that Virginia state officers had violated their oaths to defend the U.S. Constitution by embracing secession and had surrendered their rights to govern. Regardless of the argument, West Virginia has remained a separate state since 1863.

Vestiges of the rancor of this bitter divorce still can be found in the form of West Virginia jokes and jabs at each other during athletic contests. Citizens of both states tend to say "good riddance." But was it?

Virginia on the eve of the Civil War was one of the largest and wealthiest states in the country. In the post-war years, vast deposits of mineral resources were discovered in West Virginia, fueling that state's economy for decades to come. Yet it has been a state chronically saddled with grinding poverty and numerous other challenges.

Would both states have been better off as one? The debate will never end, but had there been no Civil War, Virginia probably would have remained united. And to think, some 1.9 million people would not be able to boast that they are from West "By God" Virginia.

Richmond Times Dispatch, July 3, 2011

5

THE CIVIL WAR SHOULD NOT
BE "CELEBRATED"

I cringe when someone says that we are "celebrating" the 150th anniversary of the Civil War, something I've been hearing a lot lately. To me, the word "celebrate" connotes a joyous event. "Commemorate," meaning to honor the memory of, is much more appropriate.

It is true that certain things coming out of the Civil War are worth celebrating. Some four million slaves received their freedom as a result of the conflict. Congress passed long-delayed legislation establishing land grant universities in every state, to which alumni of Virginia Tech and Virginia State University can be grateful. Our country possibly was saved from eventually disintegrating into a conglomeration of balkanized nation states.

These were positive byproducts of the war, but at what cost? If we were to put a dollar figure on the war's cost, experts estimate slightly more than $6 billion, or $2.5 million a day. Converting that figure to present value, the bill for the Civil War comes to $84.5 billion. Although that is a large sum, it pales in comparison to another cost.

How much is a human life worth? Anyone who dares to put a dollar value on it is treading in a philosophical and theological quagmire. Perhaps the best way to answer that question is to ask the mother or father, the son or daughter, the brother or sister, the husband or wife of someone who died in war. How much would they be willing to pay to get their loved ones back?

The Civil War's cost in lives is almost beyond comprehension for us. Counting deaths by combat and disease, some 620,000

Americans -- Union and Confederate -- who went off to war did not survive. If we were to convert that figure to the same percentage of today's population, that number jumps to an astonishing six million lives, equivalent to the losses of Germany, France, and Great Britain in World War I.

Visitors to the Vietnam Memorial Wall in Washington, with its nearly 60,000 names engraved on the surface, cannot help but get a sense of the enormity of that war's cost to the nation. Imagine, however, if we were to erect a similar wall to those who died in the Civil War. Such a wall would have to be stacked up another seventy-four times, adjusted to the country's current population.

Those military deaths, however, do not tell the whole story. Historians estimate that more than 50,000 civilians died during the war as a result of disease spread by the armies, guerrilla warfare, and multiple other causes.

As historian Drew Faust has noted, the Civil War "produced carnage that often has been thought reserved for the combination of technological proficiency and inhumanity characteristic of a later time."

Historians have long debated whether this national tragedy could have been prevented. Many contend that the war was an unnecessary bloodletting brought on by grandstanding extremists and blundering politicians. Kenneth Stampp argued some twenty years ago that "politicians in both sections kept the country in constant turmoil and whipped up popular emotions for the selfish purpose of winning elections. Irresponsible agitators generated hatreds and passions that made the rational settlement of differences almost impossible." How easy it would be to apply Stampp's analysis to today's environment of politics and radio talk show screeds.

One could argue that the inability of elected officials to act for the good of the republic some 150 years ago resulted in our nation's greatest tragedy. The lyrics of a heart-wrenching song of the time, "The Vacant Chair," help explain why the horrific result of their failure was not an event to celebrate for more than half a million families:

We shall meet, but we shall miss him.
There will be one vacant chair
We shall linger to caress him.
While we breathe our ev'ning prayer.
At our fireside, sad and lonely,
Oft will the bosom swell.
At remembrance of the story,
How our noble Willie fell.
How he strove to bear our banner.
Thro' the thickest of the fight.
And uphold our country's honor
In the strength of manhood's might.
True they tell us wreaths of glory,
Evermore will deck his brow,
But this soothes the anguish only,
Sweeping o'er our heartstrings now.
Sleep today o'early fallen,
In thy green and narrow bed.
Dirges from the pine and cypress
Mingle with the tears we shed.

Richmond Times Dispatch, February 13, 2011

6

CHOOSING SIDES: VIRGINIA PAID A HIGH
PRICE FOR JOINING THE CONFEDERACY

"Only the dead have seen the end of war," Plato was said to write. Although its participants are long dead, the Civil War seems to be alive and well. Governor Bob McDonnell's recent proclamation designating Confederate Heritage Month, followed by an apology for slavery, has once again stirred heated emotions. Ironically, the controversy is a vestige of a debate that raged in Virginia nearly 150 years ago.

With the election of Abraham Lincoln as president in 1860, and the subsequent secession of the states of the lower South,

Virginians faced a dilemma. Should they side with the slaveholding states of the new Confederacy or remain in the Union? For months Virginia Unionists held sway. They argued that it would be a terrible mistake to join the new cause. Secessionists preached a strident message of the dangers of remaining in the Union. Many warned that President Lincoln would destroy the institution of slavery. With Virginia being the largest slaveholding state of all and with an economy fueled in part by a lucrative slave trading business, this was no idle threat.

After the firing on Fort Sumter and Lincoln's subsequent call for volunteers to crush the Southern rebellion, Virginia soon cast its fate with the Confederacy. Within weeks, the Confederate capital was moved to Richmond, much to the delight of most Virginians. One Unionist, however, made the prescient observation that "we have a dark future in view."

Even he could not understand how dark that future would be. Virginia's contribution to the Confederate war effort was enormous. In addition to providing Richmond's industrial might, the Old Dominion supplied more generals to the Southern army than any state, as well as more troops than any other, save one.

The price it paid in treasure, human suffering, and physical destruction, however, was dear. Virginia became the great battleground of the war; the bloodiest piece of real estate in the Western Hemisphere. After Virginia left the Union in 1861, forty-one pro-Union Western counties in turn seceded and formed the new state of West Virginia. By 1865, the Virginia landscape was littered with tens of thousands of graves, burned-out homes, denuded forests, destroyed bridges, bankrupt railroads, and untilled farm land, and much of Richmond left a smoldering ruin. Those who had preached secession to protect slavery now saw that institution abolished.

Counterfactual history (looking at the past counter to what actually happened) is always tricky. I have long wondered, however, how history would have been altered had the Unionists prevailed and Virginia remained "neutral" like its neighbor Kentucky. It could be argued that without Virginia, the lifespan of the Confederacy would have been shortened and the cost in lives substantially lower. And although Virginia may have suffered a small scale internal civil war like other border states, it probably would not have become the great killing ground that it did. Richmond more than likely would not have suffered much, if any, physical destruction. Perhaps it would have thrived. Slavery would have been greatly weakened as an institution, and probably would not have survived many more years.

In retrospect, Virginia's Unionists may have had it right. Having grown up in the South, the descendant of slaveholders and Confederate veterans, I have found the celebration of the Confederacy increasingly anachronistic and less in tune with today's world. As Frederick Douglass proclaimed after the war: "There was a right side and a wrong side in the late war, which no sentiment ought to cause us to forget."

If I were in the place of my Southern ancestors 150 years ago, I, too, probably would have worn a gray uniform. But if I could have known then what I know now, my decision would have been different. By supporting the Confederacy, not only would I have been fighting on the losing side, I would have been fighting on the wrong side. If the South had gained its independence, slavery probably would have remained alive for many more years, continuing to condemn both blacks and whites to a way of life antithetical to the principles of the Declaration of Independence and a truly free republic.

I also shudder to think of the fate of the world in the twentieth century if this nation had been divided and, therefore, weaker. A United States, however, became the great Arsenal of Democracy and played a crucial role in halting Hitler's mad dream of a new world order, in blunting Japanese imperial expansion in the Far East, and eventually bringing the Soviet Union to its knees.

Frederick Douglass was correct. The right side won the Civil War. That is something worth remembering and celebrating.

Richmond Times Dispatch, April 13, 2010

7

CIVIL WAR AND THE PRICE OF FREEDOM

No conflict in American history can match the carnage of the Civil War. Approximately 620,000 men died, almost one of every four who served. Many historians now claim that figure is too low.

How does that equate to today's population? After ten years of fighting in Afghanistan and Iraq, American fatalities have numbered more than 6,200. Using comparable death rates based on the total U.S. population, the toll today for the Civil War would be 6 million in only four years.

Two key factors explain why the war killed Americans on a scale never seen before or since -- outdated tactics confronting modern weapons, and ignorance about the treatment of disease and wounds.

Civil War generals were schooled in tactics perfected by Napoleon earlier in the nineteenth century. They learned to mass their infantry in tightly packed formations and attack on a narrow front. If losses were not heavy, their men could break through enemy lines like a sledgehammer.

This tactic was based on the use of short-range, single-shot smoothbore muskets that had an effective range of a hundred yards and smoothbore artillery pieces. In 1861, both sides were armed mostly with smoothbores, yet within a year, the armies began to replace their old weapons with new rifled muskets and cannon.

The result was a dramatic increase in accuracy and range, which in turn led to much heavier casualties. In the hands of well-trained soldiers, these new weapons could hit opponents at distances four to five times that of smoothbores. Toward the end of the war, many units acquired repeating rifles that fired at a rate three times greater than single-shot muskets.

Although generals modified infantry tactics in response, they never fully changed their approach to battle. Despite overwhelming evidence that the old methods rarely succeeded, even great commanders such as Lee, Grant and Sherman relied on massed-infantry assaults well into the war, resulting in wholesale slaughter for the attackers.

While Civil War soldiers most feared enemy shot and shell, invisible killers were far more deadly. For every man killed in combat, two died of illness or disease. Dysentery, typhoid, measles and pneumonia devastated the ranks.

The makeup of the armies, North and South, reflected the mostly rural and diffuse American population then. The new soldiers had rarely congregated in large groups in confined spaces. Relatively few had been exposed to common communicable diseases, making them easy prey for the deadly microbes to which many of their urban-raised comrades were immune.

Unfortunately, Civil War-era doctors were ignorant of germs and viruses. They did not understand the need to wash their hands and medical instruments to prevent infections, which often killed soldiers rather than their wounds.

Wounds to the extremities of the body usually resulted in amputations without anesthesia or proper cleansing of the affected limb. Care of patients was frequently conducted in homes, churches, schools and barns that were hastily converted into hospitals with little regard for sanitation.

For the men who died, the loved ones left behind suffered in numbers even greater. Parents, wives, children, siblings and close friends anxiously awaited word after each major engagement, knowing "their boy" had been in harm's way. There were no official protocols to soften the blow for families. The dreaded news might come by letter from a commanding officer or a comrade in arms, sometimes months later. Newspapers published unadorned casualty lists. Often the news came by word of mouth.

For many families, information about their soldier's fate never came. Their loved one had marched off to war, only to vanish without a trace.

Because soldiers were not issued any form of identification, nearly 250,000 of the dead were never accounted for. Many were hastily tossed into mass graves after a battle, while others were never interred. As a result, their families were plunged into grief and deprived the certainty and closure that a body provides.

In her remarkable book, *This Republic of Suffering*, historian Drew Faust notes that the war left a scar on America that has never fully healed. It's little wonder. How can a people forget the pain inflicted by such a vast slaughter?

As we near the end of the first year of the Civil War sesquicentennial, we should not forget the huge price in blood this nation paid to remain united and to make all Americans free. Was it worth it? The words of a great soldier and student of the Civil War, Dwight D. Eisenhower, seem appropriate: "I hate war as only a soldier who has lived it can, only as one who has seen its brutality, its futility, its stupidity."

That said, what we must pay for something as precious as freedom often comes at a staggering price in human lives.

Richmond Times Dispatch, February 5, 2012

—∞—

8

How the Confederacy Ruled
by Big Government

I t was a central government that incurred massive debt while imposing heavy taxes on its citizenry. It had a virtual monopoly on foreign trade. It maintained *de facto* control over raw materials, labor, transportation systems and much of the manufacturing sector. It mushroomed into a huge bureaucracy to keep these controls in effect.

Was it Franklin Roosevelt's New Deal or perhaps a country under socialist rule? In reality, it was the Confederate States of America.

One of the Civil War's great ironies is that the Confederacy was formed with the belief that states' rights were supreme; yet the new government ran roughshod over that very principle. It did so in an attempt to achieve victory in war.

As historian Emory Thomas has noted, "If the South had lived in peace, the new government probably would have served the interests of the sovereign states."

Instead, during most of its existence the Confederacy was in a state of total war. As a result, by happenstance and by design, the new republic was marked by profound centralization and nationalization.

President Jefferson Davis and the Confederate Congress instituted policies designed to win a war, not protect state and individual rights. From the start, Davis insisted that state troops muster into the Confederate Army and come under the centralized control of the War Department. In April 1862, to bolster the ranks of the army he signed into law and then rigorously enforced an unpopular draft, the first ever in North America.

He often invoked martial law in parts of the Confederacy, allowing military commanders to make arbitrary arrests, control travel and fix prices in the name of national security.

Congress authorized the military to seize property from private citizens. Food, forage, livestock, and even slaves, were impressed by the army with the uncertain assurance that the Confederate government would pay for them.

The Confederacy tried desperately to finance the war at first by issuing bonds and printing inflated paper money, to little avail. By early 1863, however, Congress chose a different method of paying for the war by introducing a graduated income tax and an "agricultural tithe" on farm crops.

These and other policies by the Confederate government resulted in vigorous dissent in the South. Strong-willed governors and state legislatures bucked at many of the policies.

Georgia Governor Joseph Brown warned that there was a conspiracy by Davis to destroy states' rights and individual liberty. Governor Zebulon Vance of North Carolina stubbornly opposed Davis, especially on the conscription laws. Texas Governor Pendleton Murrah refused to send state troops to fight in the East, arguing that they were needed at home.

The ultimate success of the Confederacy depended on a strong base of support from civilians and soldiers. The soldiers performed well until the last year of an unwinnable war, when desertions increased dramatically.

Civilians, on the other hand, began to lose their faith in the cause much earlier, as military setbacks mounted and more unpopular Confederate government policies were imposed on the public. The vocal pronouncements of opposing southern authorities contributed as well.

In a remarkable speech in 1864 that echoed this discontent, Confederate Vice President Alexander Stephens cited Patrick Henry's "give me liberty or give me death" speech. He warned Southerners that they should never view liberty as "subordinate to independence." To do so would be a "fatal delusion."

To Stephens, the essence of Confederate patriotism rested on an unyielding commitment to traditional states' and individual rights. By allowing Davis's policies to continue, he believed the president would have more power than the unchecked authority of King George III prior to the American Revolution. Stephens concluded his remarks by breaking publicly with the Davis administration.

It can be argued that the Confederacy died of states' rights despite the actions of Jefferson Davis. Lack of a united front in the South, as opposed to a more cohesive Union effort, probably contributed to ultimate Confederate defeat.

Some historians have argued that the absence of a functioning two-party political system within the Confederacy hurt the cause because it did not allow for an effective alternative to Davis's policies.

Historian Bruce Catton observed that a "modern war," like the Civil War, "never goes quite where the men who start it intend it to go." Such conflicts "destroy the old bases on which society stood" and "become so all-encompassing and demanding that the mere act of fighting it changes the conditions under which men live."

No better example of that phenomenon can be found than studying the life and death of the Confederate States of America.

Richmond Times Dispatch, October 28, 2012

9

WHOSE SIDE WAS GOD ON?
CIVIL WAR RELIGION

F reedom of religion in America is a priceless right we enjoy, as is separation of church and state. When religion and politics have comingled, however, the results often have been regrettable.

Recently, some politicians publicly urged preachers to become more politically engaged. These pleas reminded me of how religion was swept up in the politics of civil war 150 years ago.

Not only did churches then impart religious values, they acted as important agents of culture, conveying civic knowledge, moral authority -- and acting as instruments of social welfare.

Although only forty percent of the country's citizens were members of organized faiths, nearly eighty percent attended church regularly. Historian Mark Noll asserts: "By 1860, religion had reached a higher point of public influence than at any previous time in American history."

The South's defense of slavery, for example, was formulated forcefully by clergymen who based their arguments on biblical validity. On the other hand, many Northern abolitionists grounded their attacks on the institution of slavery by citing the Scriptures.

Disagreements over this issue led to splits into Northern and Southern factions of the Baptist, Methodist and Presbyterian churches before the war. These divisions were a precursor of things to come -- and contributed to the eventual dissolution of the Union.

For example, most Southern clergymen supported secession, and once war began, they proclaimed their full backing of

the Confederacy. Preachers presumed the assistance of God in the
conflict, certain that the South was morally superior to the materi-
alistic, immoral North.

An Episcopal bishop in Georgia argued that the Confederacy was on a crusade to destroy the "infidel and rationalistic
principles" of misguided Yankees who were attempting to substitute a "gospel of stars and stripes for the gospel of Jesus Christ." A
Presbyterian minister in Tennessee declared that "Jesus Christ and
all his apostles were Southern men, save one. That was Judas, a
vile Massachusetts Yankee."

Early in the war, Confederate General P.G.T. Beauregard
suggested that churches donate their bells to the government to
turn them into much-needed cannon. Within weeks, bells from
throughout the South were shipped to the Tredegar Ironworks
and other factories in Richmond to be recast into bronze artillery
pieces. Thus metal once used to call worshipers to church was converted into instruments of death.

In the North, most religious bodies ardently supported the
war for the Union. A common theme advanced by Northern clergy
emphasized the Union's preservation because of America's special
place in world history. With its republican institutions, democratic
ideals and Christian values, the United States was the leader of the
civilized world. If the Confederacy succeeded in destroying the
Union, the future of humanity was jeopardized. One preacher suggested that Northern victory might prepare the way for the King-
dom of God on Earth.

Whose side was God on? Perhaps Abraham Lincoln answered that question best in his second inaugural address in March
1865.

Arguing that there were no unbridgeable differences between Northerners and Southerners, the president observed: "Both
read from the same Bible, and pray to the same God; and each
invokes His aid against the other. ... But let us judge not that we
not be judged. The prayers of both could not be answered; that of
neither has been fully answered."

With the defeat of the Confederacy, many people, North and South, argued that it was God's will. The price paid by Southern churches was heavy. As Southern morale slumped at the end of the war, religious ardor cooled. Membership in churches suffered drastic losses.

And the war played havoc on regular church activities, especially in areas heavily traversed by the contending armies. Churches often were converted into army hospitals, barracks and even stables.

It was not unusual to find houses of worship totally wrecked and stripped of their contents. By war's end, many Southern churches were virtually bankrupt.

In areas of the South where divisions were deep over national loyalty, such as East Tennessee, Western North Carolina, and Southwest Virginia, scores of congregations experienced serious rifts.

Although one of the chief tenets of Christianity is absolution, there was little forgiveness in these churches following the war. A Baptist association near Knoxville, for example, declared "non-fellowship" for any ministers and church members who had "aided or abetted willingly the past wicked rebellion against the government of the United States."

Since the Vietnam War, most American churches have either opposed armed conflict or at least not embraced it as their Civil War forbears did. I doubt that many, if any, churches today would contribute a single bell to make weaponry. Or would they if exhorted by a persuasive political figure?

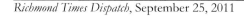

Richmond Times Dispatch, September 25, 2011

10

Gettysburg's Dark Secret:

Lee's Army and the

Order to Kidnap Freedmen

With this week's 150th anniversary of the battle of Gettysburg, we will be reminded of that epic struggle's famous highlights -- the missed Confederate opportunity to achieve victory on the first day, the struggle for Little Round Top on day two and the battle's dramatic climax on July 3 with Pickett's Charge.

The cost in lives and wounded was horrendous, with combined casualties totaling more than 50,000 men. Labeled the "high water mark of the Confederacy," the Gettysburg campaign was a turning point in the war. Never again would General Robert E. Lee mount an offensive into the North.

A closer examination of the historical record has uncovered a dark aspect of the battle that, until recently, was little known. After poring through numerous letters, diaries and the official correspondence of Confederate soldiers, historian David G. Smith reveals that as the Army of Northern Virginia moved into Pennsylvania in late June 1863, it began to round up scores of free blacks and escaped slaves to be sent south.

Lee had issued orders that the property of white citizens was to be respected during the invasion. But loosely defined, the directive enabled soldiers to capture people of color and send them to Virginia as if they were fugitive slaves. As a result men, women and children, both escaped slaves and blacks who had been born free, were grabbed by Lee's men wherever they went.

Fear spread rapidly through the African-American community in Pennsylvania when the mighty Confederate army approached. Some black residents were able to hide and avoid capture by the rebels. Most, however, fled to Harrisburg and Philadelphia, many never to return to their homes.

Nearly all of Chambersburg's pre-war black population of 1,800 fled or were captured by Lee's troops. The town of Gettysburg listed 186 African-American residents in 1860, a number that was reduced by two-thirds after the Confederate army left the area in retreat. Professor Smith estimates as many as 1,000 unlucky captives were taken to Virginia, where they were claimed by their former owners, sold at auction or imprisoned.

Did Lee know about these large-scale abductions? The Confederate general's highest ranking corps commander, James Longstreet, issued orders that authorized the action. Although that does not prove Lee sanctioned the practice, it seems unlikely he was unaware of it or that he tried to stop it.

Why did Lee's army carry out a practice akin to kidnapping? In part, it was a form of revenge. For years, slave owners in Virginia were angered over the large number of slaves who had escaped to a welcome haven in Pennsylvania, never to return to their masters.

That resentment intensified when President Lincoln issued the Emancipation Proclamation in fall 1862, which motivated slaves to flee to the North or behind Union lines in the South, further threatening the South's economy and social structure.

In addition, the formation of regiments of "U.S. Colored Troops," composed of escaped slaves and free blacks, infuriated white southerners. The thought of black men in Union uniforms was considered an unforgiveable insult.

In spring 1863, the Confederate Congress contemplated legislation authorizing the execution of captured black soldiers and their white officers. The proposal was never put into force, but the lawmakers authorized President Jefferson Davis to take "full and ample retaliation" against the North for arming former slaves.

The Civil War destroyed hundreds of thousands of lives and disrupted the social fabric of the nation. Union armies invading the South exacted a heavy toll on civilians in the destruction of property, seizure of crops and livestock -- and by offering sanctuary to slaves. Southern whites developed a deep-seated anger and hatred of Yankees, creating a resentment that was passed from one generation to another well after the war's end.

In contrast to the complaints lodged against federal armies by most of the southern populace, the Army of Northern Virginia has long been commended for its behavior during the Gettysburg campaign, thanks in part to Lee's orders to respect the white citizenry and their property. But as is often the case in studying war from our current perspective, one doesn't have to dig deeply to find its ugly aspects.

As we commemorate the epic Gettysburg campaign, new evidence that the invading Confederate army carried out a policy akin to kidnapping should not be left out of the narrative.

"The tragedy of war is that it uses man's best to do man's worst," wrote the famous preacher Henry Emerson Fosdick, a dictum that applies in every sense to the Gettysburg campaign.

Richmond Times Dispatch, June 30, 2013

11

Literate Citizen Soldiers Helped Write History of the Civil War

Why is the Civil War the most studied subject in American history? The answers are many, but one key factor is that it has all of the right ingredients for a compelling narrative -- suspense, tragedy, triumph, heroes and villains, winners and losers. It is the story of Cain and Able writ large. For a century-and-a-half the war has been told and retold by scores of gifted writers relying on a treasure-trove of written and visual source material not produced in previous wars.

The telling of the Civil War saga began with the participants themselves. High ranking officers on both sides were required to write after-action reports providing their first-hand accounts of recent battles. As soon as armed conflict ended, this massive assemblage of Confederate and Union reports was carefully gathered and compiled by the War Department. These documents were eventually published as *The Official Records of the War of the Rebellion* in one hundred twenty-eight thick volumes that provide the most comprehensive reference source on the war.

In addition, common soldiers produced an enormous quantity of letters and diaries during the war and thousands of memoirs afterwards, more so than any previous American conflict. This profusion of written information is the dividend of a dream of the Founding Fathers -- an educated citizenry.

By the middle of the nineteenth century, the literacy levels in America were such that a large percentage of soldiers on both sides of the line produced a rich harvest of written material recording their experiences in the greatest event in their lives. "Civil

War armies were the most literate in all history to that time," notes historian James McPherson.

Unlike later wars when soldier letters were heavily censored, Civil War correspondence is unadulterated. It is remarkable for showing the size and scale of the conflict, how men from farms and small towns marched off to war, why they felt compelled to fight for their respective causes -- and how conscious they were of being swept up in a grand, often fearsome and horrible, adventure.

In addition to being America's first literate war, the Civil War was the first truly visual war. No previous conflict in history had been recorded visually in such a variety of media and in such large volume. By 1861, engraved images appeared regularly in newspapers. Although crude by our standards, these images gave people some idea of what the leading figures looked like and provided a graphic concept of battle scenes.

It was not the first war to be photographed, but the Civil War generated photographic images that far outnumbered the handful that had been produced in the Mexican-American and Crimean wars. Photographs of the dead at Gettysburg, of Lee and Grant, of the ruins of Richmond in April 1865 and scores of others have become some of the most important iconic symbols in American history.

Even after the guns fell silent in 1865, the war continued to be portrayed visually and recounted in word. Artists produced a voluminous number of images of battle scenes, naval engagements and almost anything else relating to the nation's biggest conflict. As the nineteenth century drew to a close, American publishing houses rolled out a steady stream of war memoirs and regimental histories. And even today, books keep coming out, thanks in part to a seemingly infinite body of source materials for historians to mine.

Massive collections of war letters, diaries, memoirs and graphic images survive in museums, libraries and archives around the nation. The major historical institutions in Richmond are home to some of the richest Civil War collections to be found anywhere. These collections keep growing. Old letters and daguerreotypes that have long languished in attics and closets continue to be donated to public institutions, fueling new research, which in turn leads to new books on a war that never lacks an audience.

There is no way of knowing how many of these Civil War treasures are still stashed away in homes, but I never cease to be amazed at what's still out there. If you have any of these items, consider turning them over to a major historical institution like the Virginia Historical Society or the Library of Virginia, where they will be secure and available for future generations.

For that matter, with the 150th anniversary of the Civil War and Emancipation approaching, the Library of Virginia, in partnership with the Virginia Sesquicentennial Commission, has launched its Legacy Project to have war-related materials digitized so that their content will be saved and made available to the public.

The soldiers who fought in America's most costly war are long gone, but their words will live on in their letters and diaries, if we make the effort to take them to safe haven. They deserve no less, especially if their stories are yet to be told.

Richmond Times Dispatch, January 2, 2011

12

CIVIL WAR MEDICINE: A LEGACY
THAT MAY SURPRISE YOU

My grandfather told me that when he was a boy, he would steal glances at a Civil War veteran sitting in church every Sunday. The man had a gaping hole in his forehead, a gruesome reminder of the violence of war. But it was also evidence that people could survive horrific wounds before the development of modern medicine. Why was that man alive, yet so many other soldiers were not so fortunate? Was it luck or the result of skilled medical practice?

The tendency is to dismiss the latter. Compared to today's standards, Civil War medicine was primitive. An estimated 620,000 soldiers died during the conflict, two-thirds from disease and huge numbers who succumbed to wounds. With no understanding of germs and little concept of proper sanitation, doctors seemed powerless, incompetent and overwhelmed by the carnage that confronted them.

Despite its brutal reputation, Civil War medical care played

a significant role in the advent of modern medicine. As medical historian George Wunderlich contends, the war "was a watershed that changed the practice of medicine to such an extent that it would never be the same. Many aspects of modern patient care that we take for granted today can trace their origins to that war."

As hostilities began, neither side was prepared for the avalanche of illness, wounds and injuries inflicted on the men in uniform. Many leaders thought the war would be short and did not believe it was necessary to establish a costly, specialized military medical component. Within a year, however, the ghastly casualties coming from the battlefields and mounting deaths from disease forced leaders to take action. Some medical advances were made, but the most significant changes were in the way care was organized and administered.

For the Union Army of the Potomac, visionary surgeon Jonathan Letterman organized and improved the flow of patient treatment from battlefield to hospital. Letterman developed a triage system of managing mass casualties by establishing aid stations, field hospitals and general hospitals. The Federals started the first ambulance corps, which accelerated transporting patients to proper care using improved horse-drawn ambulances, specially equipped rail cars and boats. Soldiers had a greater chance to survive their wounds than they had in previous wars. Hospitals became cleaner, airier and more efficient. The ward system, which segregated patients by type of injury or illness, was established and resulted in specialized care such as orthopedics and the treatment of head injuries.

Doctors were required to keep records and make detailed reports, providing patients with a medical history, a practice that became standard procedure in civilian medicine after the war. The Confederacy organized its medical services faster than the Union, but it was plagued by limited resources throughout the war. It also did not establish a system of hospitals like the North. Hundreds of hospitals sprung up throughout the South as needed and were forced to move when Union armies approached.

By mid-1862, Richmond had become a vast medical center because of so many nearby battles. Hospitals dotted the city landscape, but one stood out. No medical facility in the Western Hemisphere equaled the size and reputation of Chimborazo Hospital on the city's east side. It became the best-organized and most sophisticated Confederate hospital, at times treating 4,000 patients. By war's end, nearly 75,000 patients had spent time at Chimborazo.

The Civil War's contributions to medical care have not been fully appreciated. The pavilion-style general hospitals were models for the large civilian hospitals of the next century. Thousands of doctors were exposed to new ideas and standards of care that proved invaluable for decades to come, including the use of anesthesia, emergency surgery and the treatment of some diseases. For the first time, female nurses were introduced in large numbers to hospital care. The U.S. Sanitary Commission was created, a civilian-controlled soldier's relief organization that set the pattern for the future Red Cross.

Civil War medicine seems unsophisticated from today's perspective. Wounded military personnel in Afghanistan have survived at much higher rates than in previous wars -- more than ninety-six percent, compared to less than eighty percent during the Civil War. Yet without the advances in medicine made during the Civil War, the number of deaths from wounds and disease would have been much greater. No doubt the man sitting in church near my grandfather was living proof of that.

Richmond Times Dispatch, July 7, 2013

13

SIR MOSES EZEKIEL:
STUDENT, SOLDIER, SCULPTOR, KNIGHT

T he Civil War profoundly affected everyone who fought in it. In one way or another, it shaped who they became. As Supreme Court Justice Oliver Wendell Holmes, Jr. later pronounced: "In our youth, our hearts were touched by fire."

There was perhaps no better example of a youth touched by war's fire than a Richmonder who went on to international acclaim as a sculptor. Born in 1844, one of fourteen Jewish children, Moses Jacob Ezekiel came from humble origins. He received a basic education but left school to work in a local store. Nevertheless, at the beginning of the Civil War, Ezekiel decided to finish his learning by attending college.

He chose the Virginia Military Institute because of its willingness to accept him despite his weak academic preparation and, as he later stated, because of his own desire to defend his native state. A member of the Class of 1866, he was the first Jew to attend VMI.

Ezekiel's cadetship was typical, yet atypical. Being Jewish, he received special attention from tormentors in the upper classes, but he later stated that he resisted their attempts at physical abuse. What distinguishes the experience of Ezekiel and his fellow cadets was an event unique in the annals of American colleges and universities.

In May 1864, a Union army under Franz Sigel moved southward through the Shenandoah Valley intending to capture Lynchburg, a vital Confederate transportation hub.

Rebel commander John C. Breckinridge assembled a make-shift army to stop Sigel. Needing every musket he could gather, Breckinridge reluctantly asked VMI Superintendent Francis H. Smith to have the cadet corps join him to serve as a reserve.

The 256 cadets, including Ezekiel, practically raced eighty-one miles to join Breckinridge near the town of New Market just as Sigel's army approached on May 15. The ensuing battle ebbed and flowed, but when Breckinridge's line wavered and a breach opened, the Confederate commander did something he had dreaded. "Put the boys in," he ordered, "and may God forgive me."

In a remarkable display of discipline and courage, the VMI lads formed up in perfect order and surged forward, Ezekiel among them. Union artillery and musket fire tore into their ranks, but the cadets kept advancing. A few minutes later when the smoke had cleared, the boys had captured a Union cannon, along with a number of blue-clad soldiers, helping turn the battle into a Confederate victory.

Ezekiel emerged from the ordeal unscathed, but the cost was heavy -- ten cadets dead or dying and forty-seven wounded. Among them was his roommate, Thomas Garland Jefferson, who died two days later in Ezekiel's arms. He never forgot that frightful experience. For the remainder of the war, Ezekiel served with other cadets training Confederate recruits and draftees in Richmond, and in the trenches of Petersburg.

In 1866, Ezekiel finished his degree at VMI. He went on to become one of the school's most distinguished graduates in a field rarely associated with his alma mater. As a cadet, he had displayed unusual artistic talent. According to some accounts, Robert E. Lee, president of neighboring Washington College after the war, urged Ezekiel to pursue those skills.

Heeding Lee's advice, Ezekiel moved to Cincinnati and then Berlin to study sculpture at the Royal Academy of Art. Once established as an artist, he moved to Rome and opened a studio.

During his career, he produced more than two hundred works and won numerous prizes and honors, including a knighthood from King Victor Emanuel of Italy.

Sir Moses never forgot his native Virginia and his alma mater. When he died in 1917 during World War I, his body was temporarily entombed in Rome. Four years later, it was interred in the Confederate Memorial section of Arlington National Cemetery. Despite his fame as an artist, his gravestone reads: "Moses J. Ezekiel, Sergeant of Company C, Battalion of Cadets of the Virginia Military Institute."

Before his death, Ezekiel donated one of his most significant works, "Virginia Mourning Her Dead," to VMI. Often referred to as the "New Market Monument," six of the ten cadets killed in battle lie near its base, including his roommate.

Eleven other statues of his can be found on the grounds of the Norfolk Botanical Garden. Exposed for years to the elements, these statues, portraying famous artists and sculptors, have been designated as some of Virginia's Most Endangered Artifacts by a program sponsored by the Virginia Collections Initiative and the Virginia Association of Museums.

How fitting it would be to restore these statues to their original glory during the Civil War sesquicentennial. Virginia's most famous artist and Civil War veteran deserves no less.

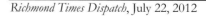

Richmond Times Dispatch, July 22, 2012

14

THE MAKING OF A SUPERIOR WARTIME LEADER (DAVIS VS LINCOLN)

I n recent years, American presidents have been judged in part by their leadership during war. Including President Barack Obama, four of the past five presidents have committed troops to combat. Only the long perspective of history enables us to fully understand how successful they were in waging war.

Is there a correlation between a president's experience in the military and his effectiveness as a wartime leader? Does personal temperament affect one's ability to lead? Which is more important—experience or temperament? The presidencies of Abraham Lincoln and Jefferson Davis during the Civil War are instructive.

From the beginning both men faced daunting tasks. On paper, it looked as if the Confederacy had chosen the superior wartime president. Davis's resume was clearly stronger than Lincoln's. A West Point graduate, distinguished Mexican War veteran, and former secretary of war, he seemed well-qualified to be an effective wartime chief executive. Indeed, as president of a disadvantaged, infant nation, Davis performed reasonably well. He forged a potent army and navy from scratch. He devised an overall military strategy that held superior federal forces at bay for four years. He transformed an agrarian economy into a relatively strong and innovative industrial force.

Nevertheless, Davis had several flaws that made him a less than ideal wartime leader. An extremely intelligent and self-confident man, he often acted as if others were not competent enough to properly carry out their duties. This led to frequent clashes with his generals, with the exception of Robert E. Lee, whom he respected. At times his strong resume was more of a hindrance than an asset. He often engaged himself in the minutia of war as exemplified by some of his first and final actions of the war. In 1861, soon after his inauguration, he spent an inordinate amount of time worrying about military equipment and accoutrements. At the end of the war, he was still signing promotions for junior officers and performing other minor tasks that were better delegated.

For his part, Lincoln appeared to stumble at first, making numerous blunders that can be blamed partially on inexperience. He initially seemed in awe of professional soldiers, some of whom in turn regarded him with disdain.

Other than a brief stint in the Illinois militia in the 1830s, Lincoln had no formal military training, but he was a quick learner and possessed an abundance of common sense. He learned and profited from experience on the job. By mid-war, he knew who his best generals were, and he let them do their jobs, intervening only when necessary. Although a Washington outsider, Lincoln soon grasped an understanding of the general organization of the federal government and how to work effectively with those in it, something Davis failed to do in Richmond.

Lincoln was humble on the surface, but in reality he was self-confident and had great persuasive and political skills. In 1861, he took charge of an office that had been occupied by weak executives for more than a decade and greatly enhanced the power of the presidency. At times he stretched his constitutional authority to its limits, arguing that those actions were necessary in order to preserve the Constitution's principles, leading to accusations that he was a tyrant.

Ironically, Davis suffered the same criticism for his actions. Like Lincoln, he was frequently hampered by the opposition of dissenters. And like Lincoln, he consolidated the powers of the central government, resulting in charges by extreme states' rights advocates that he was a dictator. More than once, he suspended the writ of habeas corpus and declared martial law to maintain civil order and loyalty to the new government.

In evaluations of the two presidents, Lincoln has received high marks from scholars. Davis has not. Even during his presidency, Davis was condemned as a failure by many of his fellow Southerners. But his defenders say his task was nearly impossible, and had their roles been reversed, Lincoln would have fared no better. That is something we will never know, but we do know Davis had certain innate flaws that prevented him from being a successful chief executive, particularly his poor people skills.

Lincoln, on the other hand, built strong alliances, did not micromanage, and used his remarkable powers of persuasion, subtle and not so subtle, to ultimately achieve victory in war.

It is worth noting that two future presidents, Franklin Roosevelt and George H.W. Bush, applied many of those skills in successfully overseeing their own war efforts. As is often the case with great leaders, temperament trumps experience.

Richmond Times Dispatch, March 20, 2011

15

HOW TIME ALTERS IMAGE:
THE CASE OF LEE AND GRANT

Does the passage of time shape our views of the past? Does it affect the way we remember things? How we perceive the life stories of two men provides an answer. One man appeared extraordinary—a distinguished family lineage, an exceptional academic record and subsequent career as a brilliant soldier. The other man seemed ordinary—a modest family background, a mediocre student, time in the army that ended unpleasantly, and then life as a civilian with an uncertain future. In early 1861, the exceptional man already was well known to the public. The other man lived in obscurity as a leather goods store clerk in Galena, Illinois

Four years later at Appomattox, however, the seemingly ordinary man, Ulysses S. Grant, accepted the surrender of the extraordinary man, Robert E. Lee. In another three years, the once-ordinary man was overwhelmingly elected president of the United States, and would serve two terms. When he died in 1883, he was one of America's most popular figures. His image appears on the $50 bill. His high standing, however, suffered over time.

Lee died in 1870 and was held in high esteem for nearly a century. Yet with the movement toward racial equality in America, Lee's reputation lost some of its luster in the eyes of many who saw the cause he defended as being on the wrong side of history.

I grew up in the South during the Civil War centennial. Lee was my hero, and I regarded Grant as the enemy. Over time, however, my perceptions changed as I closely studied the war and its aftermath. Through my own scholarship, and that of other historians, I began to understand how America's deadliest conflict has been perceived in memory from one generation to another. The winning side doesn't necessarily control how history is interpreted.

Historian David Blight argues that the dominant views of the war were the result of an extensive and skillfully conducted campaign in the late nineteenth century to portray the Confederacy in positive light.

By getting the upper hand in the "memory war," white southern writers developed a "cult of the Lost Cause," arguing that slavery was not a root cause of the war. Furthermore, the South honorably defended itself against overwhelming odds, and white southerners were the victims of a harsh and vindictive reconstruction.

Blight then notes that most white Americans accepted this version of the past, one that was reinforced by popular films such as *Birth of a Nation* and *Gone with the Wind.*

The images of the two principal military figures of the war were also molded to fit this interpretation—the noble Lee, who fought brilliantly but finally succumbed to "butcher" Grant.

Perceptions of Lee and Grant as heroes or villains are sometimes the subject of debate today. Vestiges of the Lost Cause viewpoint remain throughout the South, but they seem to be diminishing.

Three years ago, the Virginia Historical Society mounted a major exhibition on Lee and Grant reflecting the latest scholarship. Written comments solicited from visitors before and after seeing the show are revealing.

Most saw Lee as a brilliant general and a good man. "He is one of the greatest men who ever lived," wrote one visitor. On the other hand, many held negative feelings toward Grant upon entering the show. "Other than death and destruction, I fail to see why Grant should receive such attention at a Virginia institution," proclaimed one man.

Yet opinions toward the Union commander changed for numerous visitors after learning more about his life story. They were particularly impressed with the lenient terms that Grant extended to Lee at Appomattox. Grant's generous conditions were appreciated by Lee and his soldiers and set the stage for a relatively mild period of reconstruction.

Most of us were taught that Reconstruction was a dark stain on American history. Yet current scholarship reveals that when compared to the aftermaths of other civil wars, the American experience seems tame.

Although the South underwent military occupation after the war, within a few years numerous former Confederate military and government officials again controlled the political process. Slavery was abolished, but it would take another century for the slaves' descendants to realize the full fruits of American democracy.

No doubt future historians will see events of our own time differently from the way we do. As the late historian John Hope Franklin observed: "The writing of history reflects the interests, predilections, and even the prejudices of a given generation."

In other words, the way we view the past is all a matter of perspective shaped by the present.

Richmond Times Dispatch, May 29, 2011

16

EXPERIENCE OUR CIVIL WAR HISTORY: THE TOP TEN SITES TO VISIT

T he Civil War was fought over a vast territory, stretching from North Carolina's Outer Banks to the deserts of Arizona.

Opposing forces clashed in some 8,000 engagements, ranging from small skirmishes to massive battles. The sites of many of those actions are overgrown or have been lost to development. You would never know, for example, that Richmond International Airport sits atop the grounds of Seven Pines, site of a major Civil War battle.

Thanks to the efforts of the National Park Service and private organizations such as the Civil War Trust, however, hundreds of the war's most important sites have been saved to help educate the public about America's most costly war. No other country has preserved and interpreted its military heritage on such a scale.

In this first year of the Civil War sesquicentennial, visitation to related sites has increased and probably will remain strong for another four years. With so many places to visit, which ones are "must-see" to gain a better understanding of the conflict?

Here are my Top ten choices:

1.   Fort Sumter (Charleston, South Carolina)

The capture of this fort by Confederate forces in April 1861 turned decades of sectional strife into civil war. Situated in the middle of Charleston harbor, the fort is accessible only by boat, but it's well worth the trip to see where the war began.

2.   Manassas (Virginia)

In the early summer of 1861, most people believed the war would be short. But when the opposing forces met here in July in the war's first big battle, a stunning Union defeat shocked the Northern public into realizing that winning the war would not be easy. A second battle fought here in August 1862 marked one of Robert E. Lee's most remarkable victories.

3.   Shiloh (Tennessee)

Arguably the best-preserved Civil War site because of its remote location, this was the first of many battles that resulted in staggering casualties (nearly 25,000). Both sides claimed victory, but the Federal army held the field, forcing the Confederates to abandon much of Tennessee and opening the way to the Deep South. Had Union commander U.S. Grant lost this battle, he might never have reached the fame that marked him as a great general.

4.   Richmond (Virginia) -- The political and economic capital of the Confederacy, the city's capture was a key component of Union strategy for four years. Two major campaigns, the Peninsula in 1862 and the Overland in 1864, spawned numerous battles nearby, turning Richmond into the most heavily fought-over city in the Western Hemisphere. Its fall in April 1865 rang the death knell for the Confederacy. A visitor could spend a week here without seeing it all.

5.   Antietam (Maryland)

This hauntingly beautiful battlefield was the site of the bloodiest day of the war. Considered a tactical draw, Antietam was a turning point. Lee's retreat to Virginia gave President Lincoln the opportunity to announce the Emancipation Proclamation in late 1862, converting the purpose of the war from an effort only to save the Union into a crusade to free the slaves. Changing public sentiment in Europe destroyed the South's last hope of foreign assistance.

6.   Gettysburg (Pennsylvania)

Union victory here in the summer of 1863 ended Lee's second invasion of the North and was a turning point in the war. This battle-

field is the most visited Civil War site of all. The new museum/
visitors center is a good place to start a tour of this epic three-day
battle. Visitors should give themselves at least two days to take it
all in.

7.   Vicksburg (Mississippi)

The town's surrender on July 4, 1863, was the culmination of
Grant's most brilliant campaign, splitting the South and giving
control of the Mississippi River to the Union. It is one of the most
heavily commemorated parks in the world, with more than 1,300
monuments, tablets and markers.

8.   Chickamauga (Georgia)/Chattanooga (Tennessee)

In 1863, opposing forces fought for Chattanooga, a crucial rail
junction known as the "Gateway to the South." Confederate victory at nearby Chickamauga in September led to a lengthy siege
of Union forces in Chattanooga. Grant broke the Confederate grip
on the city in November, opening the way to Atlanta in 1864. The
view from Lookout Mountain is spectacular.

9.   Petersburg (Virginia)

After months of brutal fighting in the spring of 1864, Union forces
under Grant backed Lee's army into defensive lines around Petersburg. The two armies were locked in a nine-month siege, punctuated by intense fighting. In April 1865, Grant flanked the Confederate line and forced Lee to retreat toward Appomattox. A full day is
needed to see the numerous sites associated with the siege, including the famous Crater.

10.   Appomattox (Virginia)

Lee's surrender to Grant at the McLean house in April 1865 sig-
naled the end of war. Grant's generous terms set the tone for a
relatively mild period of reconstruction when compared to the
aftermaths of other civil wars. Appomattox will be home next year
to a new museum operated by the Museum of the Confederacy.

A final word of advice: Try to visit these sites near the time of year the actions occurred to gain a better understanding of the events. Seeing Gettysburg with snow on the ground, for example, makes it harder to imagine what happened in July 1863.

Richmond Times Dispatch, December 4, 2011

Part II

Virginia

AND THE

American South

I have always lived in the South. I was born and raised in Tennessee, and have lived at one time or another in Alabama, Georgia, Kentucky, Missouri, and now Virginia. Between my four years of college and the last twenty-seven years in Richmond, 40 percent of my life has been spent in Virginia.

Having lived throughout the South, I have noticed that state pride is especially strong in the region, but it varies from one state to another. Alabamians are proud of their college football teams. Kentuckians boast of their bourbon whiskey, horseracing, or Kentucky Wildcat basketball. With Tennesseans, pride seems to rest as much with its three grand divisions—East, Middle, and West Tennessee—as it does with the state as a whole.

It did not take me long, however, to learn that there is a distinctive pride among Virginia natives. Some would say it is hubris. William Faulkner is reputed to have said: "I like Virginians because they're snobs, and I like snobs."

They have good reason to be snobs when it comes to history. I cannot think of another state that has a past that is as colorful and rich as Virginia's. It is a history so interwoven with American history that in many ways it is the centerpiece of the national narrative.

Virginia is a paradox. It was the first British colony to import slaves, but later it sired the authors of the Declaration of Independence, the U.S. Constitution, and the Bill of Rights. One of its native sons, General George Washington, led the forces that won independence for the United States, yet 80 years later another Virginian, Robert E. Lee, fought for its dissolution. It resisted federal government social programs during the New Deal and civil rights legislation, but it gladly accepted the billions of federal dollars that flowed into the state from defense-related activities. It was one of the last states to integrate its public colleges and universities, yet it elected the nation's first African-American governor.

All of those things make Virginia's past such a rich subject to study. As I eventually learned, one would be hard pressed to find a better environment for a historian to live and work.

17

SOUTHERN FOOD AND
AMERICAN CULTURE

A s I read the menu at a swanky New York restaurant recently, three items brought back memories of my childhood in rural Tennessee. "Turnip Greens and Polenta Napoleon," "Curry Okra Souffle," and "Fancy Mixed Berry Cornbread Dressing" were not things I expected to find in mid-town Manhattan, nor did they resemble the turnip greens, fried okra and cornbread served to me half a century ago.

Their presence on the menu, however, reflects significant changes in American cuisine and eating habits. My grandmothers and my mother were excellent cooks, but the fare they served was based on cooking techniques, ingredients and recipes that had changed little over decades.

Even now, my mouth waters at the memories of hot biscuits and cornbread, of vegetables cooked slowly in a pot on a stove top, and golden-brown chicken fried in a big, black skillet, of cobbler loaded with berries picked that morning.

Pizza, tacos, arugula salad, sweet and sour pork, orzo, fresh seafood, fresh vegetables year-round, and a host of other items that are now standard items in the American diet were practically unheard of when I was young.

My first pizza came out of a Chef Boyardee box -- and tasted suspiciously like its cardboard packaging. Every once in a while, my mother served chicken chow mein, which was an exotic Asian dish to us. Little did we realize that this prepared meal from cans had been developed in San Francisco to appeal to the mild American palate.

"The South, for better or worse, has all but lost its identity as a separate place . . . but its food survives," noted writer John Egerton 25 years ago. Since then, Southern cuisine not only survives, it appears on menus and family dinner tables far from Dixie. Thanks in part to cable television's star chefs like Paula Deen and the national chain of Cracker Barrel restaurants, dishes once limited to the South can be found almost anywhere. Barbeque, once an exclusively southern meat specialty, can be had in London. One thing hasn't changed, however. In the South, the word barbeque is a noun, as in "I love to eat barbeque." In the North, it is a verb: "Let's go barbeque some burgers."

The geographic expansion of foods should come as no surprise to a historian like me. In reality it has been going on for thousands of years. Probably the best example of this phenomenon is what historians label the Columbian Exchange.

Within a matter of years following Christopher Columbus's 1492 voyage to America, a widespread exchange of animals, plants, food, culture, human populations, animals, diseases and ideas between the Eastern and Western hemispheres began. Our cuisine today is closely tied to the Columbian Exchange.

Before 1492, there were no oranges in Florida, no bananas in Central America, no potatoes in Ireland, no tomatoes in Italy, no pineapples in Hawaii, no paprika in Hungary and no chocolate in Belgium.

In addition to improving the quality and variety of European cuisine, this exchange had profound, long-term effects. With the introduction of food such as potatoes and corn, Europeans had longer and healthier lives. As a result, Europe experienced a steady growth in population and an agricultural revolution involving new methods of crop production.

But I digress from the subject of Southern cuisine. Food by whatever its name --country cooking, home cooking, soul food -- has played a crucial role in the South's social and cultural history. It has also affected the region's medical history.

Health experts have long recognized that despite its many wonderful qualities, the Southern diet is not a model of proper eating. Fried foods, vegetables simmered to a fare-thee-well with salt pork, country ham, biscuits and gravy, and pie crusts made with lard may be pleasing to the palate, but they are devastating over time to one's cardiovascular system. It is little wonder that the South has long led the nation in heart attacks and strokes.

Nevertheless, I, like many Southerners, occasionally find myself yearning for those old dishes. As John Egerton observed, "food is the only element that reaches our consciousness through all five senses. Such a powerful force is bound to linger in our memory."

Last year, as I watched the scene of Minny Jackson teaching her white protege, Celia Foote, how to fry chicken in the film *The Help*, I felt my stomach growling and my hunger pangs increasing.

Although my wife and I had kept that item out of our diet for years, we stopped on the way home to buy chicken and a can of Crisco. Once home, I found our long-stored cast iron skillet, set it on the stovetop with a large dollop of Crisco, while my wife shook the chicken pieces in a brown grocery sack filled with flour.

Soon the chicken pieces popped and sizzled in the skillet and turned golden brown. The result was a meal worthy of any of New York's finest restaurants.

Richmond Times Dispatch, November 18, 2012

18

AIR CONDITIONING AND HOW
IT CHANGED THE SOUTH

Polite people referred to it as perspiration, but no matter what you call it, sweat flowed freely from anyone who experienced a summer day in the South more than 50 years ago. In cities productivity fell dramatically. Office work was a stifling experience, and in many places business simply melted away. The federal government went into a lengthy siesta when elected officials and bureaucrats fled the nation's steamy capital. People who traveled by car felt as if they were riding in an oven on wheels. The sermons in church always seemed longer in August as the only salvation from the heat was paper funeral home fans that waved furiously back and forth.

Such experiences are foreign to most people born in the past quarter of a century because they have lived in an air-conditioned bubble for most of their existence. While we may regard it simply as another luxury added to the long list of those Americans enjoy, we often overlook the profound economic, social, demographic, and political implications of artificially cooled air.

Since ancient times, people have tried to keep themselves cool, designing buildings and clothing to adapt to warm climates. Nineteenth-Century inventors devised a number of contraptions to beat the heat, and in 1882 the new electric fan was hailed as the answer to surviving summers. Still, no one had discovered a way to conquer the smothering humidity that blanketed a summer day. The precise relationship between moisture content and temperature was not understood. Why does a humid, 85-degree day in Richmond seem more oppressive than a 95-degree day in Phoenix?

New York engineer Willis Carrier finally discovered the clues that had been staring people in the face for centuries. He developed a mechanical device that created an artificial fog by spraying a fine mist of water into a box, thus saturating the air inside. By adjusting the temperature of the water supply, he could control the temperature of the air. Because cold air holds less moisture than warm, he could regulate the humidity as well. In effect, he learned to wring the excess moisture from the air passing through his apparatus by using water particles from the spray as a condensing surface. In 1902, Carrier installed his first system in a lithographic company in Brooklyn that had been forced to suspend operations when humidity levels became too high.

Air conditioning started in the North, but its fastest growth took place in the South. Several textile mills in the Carolinas installed massive systems, not for the comfort of the workers, but to better control moisture content in the fibers they worked with. Within a decade, Carrier's invention moved into tobacco factories, paper mills, breweries, bakeries, and other industries.

By the 1920s, Carrier and several competitors pushed for a much wider application of air conditioning. They worked constantly to make systems smaller, more efficient, safer, cheaper, and more for the comfort of people. Movie palaces in major cities led the way. Theaters in Richmond enticed customers with frost-covered signs boasting, "20 Degrees Cooler Inside." Department stores, hotels, and banks followed suit in the 1930s, as did a handful of hospitals and government buildings.

Despite the growing industrial and commercial use of air conditioning, most Americans had little exposure to artificially cooled air in their homes. World War II hastened its industrial application, but with the return of peace it spread at an even faster rate. For the first time in years, Americans had disposable income. They purchased homes, automobiles, furniture, televisions, refrigerators, and now-affordable commercial and residential air conditioners as never before. In the 1950s the number of air-conditioned homes in the South quadrupled. Air conditioning, which at first was limited to luxury cars, gradually became standard equipment even in most economy models.

Most of us take air conditioning for granted, but its effect on altering our character, particularly in the South, has been profound. It has reshaped the nation's economy and demographics. The great migrations, the industrial development, and urbanization in the Sun Belt would not have been possible without it. Between 1900 and 1950, the South experienced a net loss of ten million people. But in the 1980s alone, the region had a net gain of nine million. Since the advent of air conditioning, many Southern states have grown at a ten-percent rate every decade. It is no coincidence that since 1950, the South has urbanized more than any other section of the country, from thirty-six percent to more than seventy-five percent in 2000. The exploding population of Florida is tied closely to the spread of air conditioning.

Some Southerners lament the loss of distinct regionalism caused in part by interstate highways, mass media, and, yes, air conditioning.

Historian Raymond Arsenault observes, "General Electric has proved a more devastating invader than General Sherman. As long as air conditioning, abetted by immigration, urbanization, and computers, continues to make inroads, the South's distinctive character will continue to diminish." One elderly Florida woman complained: "I hate air conditioning. It's a damn-fool Yankee invention. If they don't like it hot, they can move back North where they belong!"

Perhaps more significant has been the effect air conditioning has had in isolating us from the natural environment and the loss of neighborliness. From ancient times until recent decades, we have been influenced by the touch of Nature. But with the growth of technology such as air conditioning, our whole outlook on the world around us has changed.

But who would want to go back to the days of working in stifling offices, riding in oven-like cars, or funeral home fans? Although some people may pine for the slower pace of languid summer days, most of us would not be willing to live outside our air-conditioned bubble. The great irony of it all is that a New York engineer's invention has made a truism of the old battle cry "the South will rise again!"

Richmond Times Dispatch, July 24, 2005

19

Rosenwald Schools:
Making Black Schools More Equal

When the United States was established, its founders proclaimed the need for an educated citizenry to ensure the success of their experiment in republican government. During the first half of the nineteenth century, schools sprang up throughout the young nation. As a result, the United States had one of the most literate populations in the world by mid-century.

From the beginning, however, some Americans could not receive the benefits of a solid education. Women, for example, did not have access to full educational opportunities until well into the twentieth century, as did American Indians.

Most African-Americans were not schooled until after the Civil War. Before the war, laws in the slave states forbade educating blacks. Concerned whites believed that literate blacks, particularly slaves, would demand freedom and foment insurrection. As one southern observer noted: "An educated Negro is a dangerous Negro."

With the end of slavery, the federal government created the Freedman's Bureau to assist the newly liberated people to become citizens. A key component of that process was education. Congress directed significant funding toward education in the post-war South—for the most part segregated education. With educational opportunities now available to them, African-Americans accepted separate schools, thus avoiding interference from and potential conflict with whites.

During its seven-year existence, the Bureau built schools, provided educational materials, and paid teacher salaries. This was the first-ever involvement of the federal government in large-scale social welfare and a precursor of programs that would be established in the twentieth century. Its achievements were significant, and by 1869, more than 3,000 new schools had been established in the South, along with numerous black colleges, the first of their kind.

They, however, depended on white controlled state and local governments for continued funding. Fearing that educated blacks would challenge white supremacy, state officials kept financial support for African-American schools at levels considerably lower than for white schools.

Most black schools were housed in shoddy, ramshackle buildings. Black teachers were paid less than their white counterparts, and many had inadequate credentials. Students often used discarded textbooks from white schools. These conditions ensured second-class citizenship for African-Americans in the South beginning at an early age.

The landmark U. S. Supreme Court decision of *Plessy v. Ferguson* in 1896 confirmed the legality of segregation in many forms, including education, as long as facilities for each race were equal. With no real means to enforce this concept of "separate but equal," non-white schools in the South remained markedly inferior for decades.

This inherent unfairness of education in the former Confederacy drew the attention of Julius Rosenwald, the son of German-Jewish parents and one of the founders of Sears, Roebuck, and Company in Chicago. When Rosenwald met Booker T. Washington in 1912, the famed African-American educator urged the wealthy businessman to help do something about the dire condition of black education.

A few years later, Rosenwald and his family created the Rosenwald Fund "for the well-being of mankind." Unlike other philanthropic foundations that are funded in perpetuity, the Rosenwald Fund proposed spending all of its assets. For the next thirty years, the Fund donated more than $70 million to public schools, colleges, museums, and a number of Jewish causes before being entirely depleted.

The school program was the largest Rosenwald initiative. To promote collaboration between the white and black communities, he required communities to match his grants with public funds and private dollars. Millions of dollars were raised in the South to construct better schools for African-Americans. Nearly 4,000 so called Rosenwald schools were built using plans developed by Tuskegee Institute professors of architecture.

By 1932, these schools accommodated about a third of all African-American pupils in the South. Subsequent studies revealed that Rosenwald schools significantly improved student attendance, test scores, and the overall educational experience.

With the depletion of the Rosenwald Fund in the late 1940's, however, the school program ended. And with the Supreme Court's 1954 decision to overturn the "separate but equal" concept of education, little by little Rosenwald schools were abandoned and fell into disrepair.

Although the number of extant Rosenwald school buildings is uncertain, one, in western Goochland County, has been saved and refurbished by a group of dedicated volunteers in collaboration with the Goochland County Historical Society. Constructed in 1918, the two room, two teacher Second Union School is the oldest surviving of ten Rosenwald schools built in the county.

Take a drive for about five miles south on Hadensville-Fife Road from I-64, and you will see a proud symbol of one man's resolve to correct a wrong, and the determination of African-Americans to become educated citizens in the face of numerous obstacles. During its lifetime, it was one small step in the long journey toward equality in America.

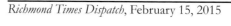

Richmond Times Dispatch, February 15, 2015

20

MANUFACTURING A NEW VIRGINIA, ONE BOX AT A TIME (LANE CEDAR CHEST COMPANY)

A seemingly insignificant event one hundred years ago symbolized a rapidly changing Virginia. In 1912, John Lane of Charlottesville bought a bankrupt wooden packing box plant in the small town of Altavista. He then turned it over to his son, Edward, to run. Within a decade, young Lane transformed a modest company into one of the largest manufacturers of cedar chests in the world.

How did he do it? Lane was both creative and a student of history. He learned that the ancient Egyptians were aware of the protective qualities of cedar chests to hold their finest garments. They also were part of a young bride's dowry, a tradition that over time spread to Europe.

Understanding the romantic connection to the cedar chest, Lane developed a bold marketing strategy to convince potential brides in Virginia and beyond that they needed a cedar chest as part of their dowry. Lane started running well-crafted advertisements in magazines with a national circulation, especially women's journals, pushing the idea that every bride needed a cedar chest.

Once this targeted marketing campaign was launched, Lane came up with a clever follow-up scheme. Over the years he had noticed many of his factory workers crafting miniature cedar chests for their girlfriends. Lane's staff compiled a massive list of girls graduating from high school and sent them certificates good for a free miniature chest at their local Lane dealers.

The initial response was overwhelming. Within a few years, nearly two-thirds of the girls graduating from American high schools received Lane certificates.

Even during the Depression, Lane chests sold well. Work shifted to defense production during World War II, but business boomed in the late 1940s and in the '50s. At its peak in the 1960s, Lane Company employed more than 2,500 workers in its Altavista plant and operated seventeen factories in five states.

Then, as would happen to many other domestic case-good manufacturers in America, the light began to dim for Lane. Rising costs, particularly labor, and overseas competition proved to be too much. The company was taken over by a St. Louis investment group in the 1980s. In 2002, the ninety-year-old plant in Altavista closed and the remnants of Lane's corporate headquarters moved to Mississippi. An important chapter in Virginia history ended.

Ed Lane and then his son B.B., and scores of other manu-facturers like them, especially in the tobacco and textile industries, were agents of change in Virginia. As more factories sprang up in towns and cities, they created jobs that offered a more lucrative alternative to farm work.

For a growing number of people, earning $5 a day in a fac-tory was preferable to barely making ends meet with backbreaking farm work. At first, it began as a trickle, but then a flood of people moved from the country to towns like Altavista, from farm to fac-tory. By the mid-twentieth century, for the first time in the state's history, most Virginians lived in towns, cities and suburbs.

Wartime accelerated the process of economic transforma-tion, with shipping and defense industries taking a firm hold in the Old Dominion. These industries became the backbone of the Virginia economy during the Cold War.

This great economic shift profoundly affected Virginia. Devastated by the Civil War, the Old Dominion finally regained its financial footing a century later. The demand for an educated work force needed in the new economy helped lead the way for better schools and universities -- and more stringent educational standards. During World War II the traditional role of women changed as more began to work outside the home.

And in some ways, the economic shift played a slow but subtle role that eventually helped break down racial segregation by creating jobs and opportunities for African-Americans that simply had not existed before in a heavily agricultural economy.

History is marked by turning points, the actions taken and decisions people made that have shaped the course of the future. Some turning points are dramatic and instantly recognizable, such as the Japanese attack on Pearl Harbor. Others, however, are more subtle and take the perspective of time to recognize.

Little did the Lane family realize a century ago that the purchase of a little wooden box company would prove to be one of those subtle but profoundly important turning points. It makes you wonder if a seemingly insignificant event today will be viewed as a turning point a century from now.

Richmond Times Dispatch, June 17, 2012

21

BOUND AWAY: VIRGINIA AND
THE WESTWARD MOVEMENT

A t one time, Virginia was Number One. Indeed, at the end of the American Revolution, no other state equaled Virginia in size, population, wealth and political influence. Yet within two decades, the Old Dominion was in trouble as its population melted away. From the pre-eminent place it had occupied since the colonial period, Virginia slipped almost into a secondary role.

Its agriculture-based economy was the chief culprit. With little knowledge of the application of fertilizer and crop rotation, farmers in the Tidewater and the Piedmont overplanted tobacco, resulting in widespread soil exhaustion. Between 1817 and 1829, Virginia land values plunged from $207 million to $90 million.

Conditions in the wheat-producing Shenandoah Valley were better, but even there people could envision a happier life outside of Virginia as they received glowing reports from friends and relatives who had moved to newer states and territories farther west.

In 1848, Branch Archer, who had settled in Texas, wrote his sisters back home: "Virginia is waning fast. ... quit her as rats quit sinking vessels, and take a home in this land of promise. ..." The words of an early 19th-century ballad, "Shenandoah," seemed fitting: "Away, I'm bound away, cross the wide Missouri."

When available land opened farther west, an estimated one million people left Virginia between the American Revolution and the Civil War, according to historians David Hackett Fischer and James C. Kelly. Nearly a third of those who departed did so involuntarily as slaves, taken by their masters or sold at high profits to planters in the emerging cotton states.

Virginia fell from first to seventh place in population by the 1830s. Its congressional representatives dropped from twenty-three to eleven.

The Commonwealth's influence on the national scene declined, but the mass exodus of Virginians had a profound effect wherever they went. Virginia culture, laws, political philosophy, labor system, surveying practices, honor concepts and architectural styles spread across America.

Virginians who played key roles in the history of the westward movement include the likes of John Sevier (Tennessee's first governor); Sam Houston and Stephen and Moses Austin in Texas; James Denver (Colorado's first territorial governor); Henry Clay; mountain man Jim Bridger; artist George Caleb Bingham; the slave Dred Scott; author Willa Cather; educator Booker T. Washington; and inventor/philanthropist Cyrus McCormick. Abraham Lincoln's grandfather was a Virginian.

After decades of decline, followed by the devastation of the Civil War, Virginia did not emerge from its malaise until the twentieth century, when economic conditions improved and opportunities returned, fueled at first by the tobacco industry and later by federal defense spending. In-migration gradually replaced out-migration.

If there is any constant in American history, it is that we are a nation of movers. People who study their family history have some sense of when their ancestors came to America. Once those forebears arrived here, they and their offspring rarely stayed in the same place.

In 1818, for example, Nelson and Polly Bryan and their children pulled up stakes in Virginia's Halifax County and moved 500 miles west to Shop Springs in Middle Tennessee. Why they left is unknown. We can only speculate that perhaps they sought new opportunities.

Nelson and Polly spent the rest of their lives on their farm near Shop Springs. But most of their children and their children's children left and continued the great folk migration. Their offspring moved elsewhere, continuing a cycle of family moves that began in Scotland and Ireland centuries before.

One of their great-grandsons (my grandfather) was born and raised on the farm at Shop Springs; but as a young man he moved to take a white-collar job in another county. There he met a young woman whose great-grandparents moved to Tennessee from Virginia. When they married in 1905, two old Virginia lines merged. And again repeating the cycle, their children and their children's children eventually left home to seek opportunities elsewhere.

Ironically, opportunity in the form of a job drew me to Virginia twenty-five years ago, bringing full circle the move my great, great, great-grandfather made from the Old Dominion nearly two hundred years ago.

Like mine, most American families have participated in part or all of four great migrations in our history -- from elsewhere to America, from east to west, from country to city, and from city to suburb.

Today, people of all backgrounds seek new opportunities no less than those who left Virginia in the early nineteenth century. The experience of immigrants coming to America, people moving in and out of our neighborhoods, from one state to another, and from one job to another is nothing new. It is a continuation of a phenomenon set in motion centuries ago, and it will continue for the ages to come.

Richmond Times Dispatch, July 6, 2014

22

VIRGINIA EXCEPTIONALISM

The term "American exceptionalism" has been in the news lately. Dating from the nineteenth century, the concept has been used to argue that the United States is "qualitatively different" from other nations. To some pundits, it implies American superiority. To others, it represents American hubris.

I have been thinking about exceptionalism and Virginia. What has made Virginia distinctive? Is it "qualitatively different?" Given the fierce pride that its natives have in their beloved commonwealth, there does seem to be a "qualitative difference."

A path-breaking synthesis of colonial America published twenty-five years ago by Pulitzer Prize-winning historian David Hackett Fischer titled *Albion's Seed: Four British Folkways in America* suggests that exceptionalism came early to Virginia. Fischer attempts to answer why certain regions of the country have different cultural characteristics that persist today and help explain our nation's collective history.

He argues that the distinctiveness of four regions of British colonial America -- New England, Virginia, the Delaware Valley and the Backcountry -- gave rise to the pluralism and libertarianism that America needed to accommodate its differences and come together to form a single nation.

Virginia paradoxically created a unique culture, yet its influence on the future nation was profound. Colonial Virginia was ruled by a small number of elite families. Fischer argues they had a firm grip on the region, ruling over a stratified society in which seventy-five percent of its people were poor indentured servants in the seventeenth century and an increasing number were slaves in the eighteenth century.

Virginia society was hierarchical, closely tied to the crown, based on systems of rank and status -- and an ideology of "hegemonic liberty." This gave the elite the power to rule over others in a place where liberties were not universal but divvied up according to rank. Distribution of wealth was heavily skewed in favor of a few families.

Ironically, Virginia was the birthplace of the authors of the Declaration of Independence, the United States Constitution and the Bill of Rights. Seven of the first twelve presidents were native Virginians. Virginia's General Assembly is the oldest representative body in the Western Hemisphere and is often referred to as the cradle of American democracy.

On the other hand, Virginia was the first English colony to introduce slavery. Its capital city became the capital of the Confederacy, and Virginia turned into the great battleground of the Civil War in large part because of the southern defense of slavery. It rose up in Massive Resistance against integrating public schools in the twentieth-century.

I talked with Professor Fischer not long ago, and we agreed that the old Virginia is giving way to a new Virginia. Is the Commonwealth losing its sense of exceptionalism? There is plenty of evidence to suggest that it is, at least in its old form.

For one, fewer people living in Virginia are born here. During the last century, Virginia experienced the largest drop in residents native to their respective states. In 1910, nearly ninety percent of the state's population was born here. A century later, less than fifty percent is composed of native Virginians, a number that continues to decline, especially in urban/suburban population clusters. Virginia's foreign-born population has grown to 11.4 percent.

Without question, this change has affected Virginia profoundly, as evident by the state's politics. Long a bastion of conservatism, whether led by Byrd Democrats or their Republican successors, Virginia has been gradually shifting to the left. Once a solid red state, it now is becoming a deeper shade of purple.

Once an agricultural-based economy that shifted to one heavily invested in manufacturing, Virginia's economy now is much more diverse. Once proud of its fierce independence from the federal government, Virginia ranks high among top states to receive federal dollars.

Virginia did not ratify the 19th amendment (guaranteeing women the right to vote, though federal law ensured they could) until 1952 and was it one of the last states to admit African-Americans and women to its public universities. Yet it became the first state to elect an African-American as its governor, and a woman now heads the University of Virginia.

Perhaps Virginians have become a "people of paradox," a description given to the American people by the late historian Michael Kammen. Noting that America was complex from the beginning, its people "have rushed individually and simultaneously in different directions."

Professor Fischer reminds us, however, that our country was founded on a "set of different and even contradictory traditions in creative tension with one another. This diversity of libertarian ideas has created a culture of freedom which is more open and expansive than any unitary tradition alone could possibly be." If that is true of Virginia, we are witnessing not the death of "Virginia exceptionalism," but rather its rebirth in a new form.

Richmond Times Dispatch, June 29, 2014

23

I Once Was Blind:

Growing Up in the Segregated South

A few years ago, I read the memoir of the late Carl Rowan, a distinguished journalist and diplomat. As I turned the pages of his book, I began to realize for the first time how ignorant I once was. Rowan and I grew up in the same small town —McMinnville in Middle Tennessee—but we never met because we lived in separate worlds. Those worlds were shaped by centuries old events—and by the fact that I am white and he was black.

Even as a little boy, I was fascinated by the past, especially the Civil War. Its vestiges were everywhere. A Confederate monument stood guard in the town square. My antebellum home was near an old encampment of Nathan Bedford Forrest's cavalry. A photograph of Robert E. Lee hung in my room. My best friend and I frequently faced off on a board game based on the battle of Gettysburg, he always playing the Union commander while I was Lee. When I fared no better than the real Lee, I went into a blue funk. I cheered for our City High Rebels—and, along with my fellow stu-

The author's grandfather Clarence Bryan shares some time with his good friend Roy Webb on a porch in Middle Tennessee in 1962.

dents, waved Confederate flags for our all-white school at athletic events.

In my simplistic understanding of history, I clearly saw the war from a white, southern perspective. To me, Confederates were the good guys, while Yankees were villains. I wistfully imagined scenarios of the South winning the war. I gave no thought to the fact that Confederate victory would have been a triumph for a nation founded in large part to preserve the institution of slavery.

I didn't consider the consequences of a divided America in the twentieth century. We know that the United States helped turn the first World War in favor of the Allies in 1917-18. It became the most powerful country on Earth after playing the lead role in defeating Nazi Germany and Imperial Japan.

Most of all, I was ignorant of the racial injustices carried over from the legacy of slavery. Jim Crow was alive and well in my hometown, and it formed the world of Carl Rowan's youth. It featured separate seating in the balcony at the local movie theater, segregated water fountains and bathrooms at the county courthouse, and seats for blacks at the back of Greyhound buses.

Even though we resided in the same community, he lived in a poor section of town with street names such as Congo or Egypt Alley. He attended all-black schools in buildings inferior to my school. Because he was denied access to the public library, a white friend surreptitiously checked out books for him. No black held public office, and I have no memory of anyone of color who was a member of the town's business or professional elite. Even the dead rested in separate cemeteries according to race.

*****

My early years in that community seem almost idyllic, but they were not for Rowan. Wanting more from life than menial jobs and second-class citizenship, he had to escape the oppressive environment of his youth to succeed. It was an environment that left him with few fond memories of his boyhood hometown.

When I read Rowan's account, I wondered if my family contributed to the system of apartheid that was smothering him, despite our somewhat enlightened views for that time. I grew up in a home where I was told that I was no better than anyone else, regardless of my skin color. The "N" word was strictly forbidden.

Before his premature death, my father, a musician and composer, had taught a gifted but untutored African-American how to sing well enough to eventually have his debut at Royal Albert Hall in London. At night, my mother taught him proper grammar and elocution. My mother never joined the Daughters of the American Revolution because they refused to allow black opera singer Marian Anderson to perform in Constitution Hall before an integrated audience in 1939.

I remember frequent visits from my grandfather's good friend, Roy Webb, an African-American. He and my grandfather spent many hours on our front porch swapping yarns.

It was the segregated South, however, and both men adhered to the social etiquette of the time. Mr. Webb always came to our back door first. He addressed my grandfather as "Mr. Clarence" and my mother as "Miss Edith." In return, they called him "Roy." I am now embarrassed to say that even as a young boy, I also called him and other African-American adults, such as our school janitors and our maids, by their first names. Because that was common practice then, I was never called to task for it by anyone, white or black.

It was only when I began to study American history in depth and had my mind opened to other viewpoints that I developed some sense of the world from Rowan's perspective. Tacitly my family and I had been agents of the injustices of the time by simply allowing them to exist. As the words of Amazing Grace proclaim, I once was blind, but now I see.

I wonder what injustices and wrongs I am blind to today? Worse yet would be to see them and do or say nothing.

* For reader reaction to this essay, see page 268.

24

FROM WAR TO WAR:
THE SOUTH ROSE SLOWLY

Occasionally I am asked what would have happened if the South had won the Civil War. I find such questions difficult to answer. Historians are trained to ground their arguments in known facts and solid evidence. To try to determine what might have happened is based on pure speculation. I usually answer the question by relating what really happened.

In the short term, the South paid an enormous price in blood and treasure for seceding from the Union and then losing the war. he long-term consequences were also profound. Although post-war reconstruction was relatively mild, the South was plunged into poverty for decades. There was little public sympathy in the North for the losing side. As a result no Marshall Plan was implemented to restore the devastated economy of the former Confederacy. Thus the South lagged badly behind the rest of the country socially and economically for nearly a century.

A snapshot of the nation in 1900 is revealing.

The northeast quadrant of the U.S. had become one of the world's great manufacturing regions. Its population was increasingly wealthy, urbanized, educated and although predominantly white, it was marked by growing ethnic, religious and cultural diversity with new waves of European immigrants.

The Northern Plains had been altered from frontier into a rich agricultural region, specializing in wheat and other grains that were exported in great quantities. The western states derived substantial wealth from mining, ranching and innovative commercial agriculture.

The picture was not so bright for the South. Considered wealthy on the eve of the Civil War, the region was the nation's poorest by 1900. Its per capita income was half of the U.S. average.

Its population was thirty-two percent black, most of whom lived in poverty. The new European immigration had little effect on the majority white population. It was a region gripped by rigid racial segregation, making some argue that southern blacks were not much better off than before emancipation. By the early twentieth century, large numbers of the region's black population were moving to northern cities in search of greater freedom and opportunity.

The South differed in other ways as well. While forty percent of the nation's population lived in urban areas and twenty-five percent of its labor force worked in factories, the South was only eighteen percent urban and a mere ten percent of its labor pool was involved in manufacturing.

The South also fell short in the mainstay of its economy. Southern agriculture suffered from relatively low productivity, undercapitalization, small financial returns and a large number of small, subsistence farms. Agriculture, once the pride of the South, had fallen on hard times.

Little by little, however, the movement of people from farm to factory, from country to city began to affect the South as well. The region changed more in the twentieth century than in the three previous centuries. The industrial revolution that started in England centuries earlier finally reached the American South.

In Virginia, for example, factories began to dot the landscape. Tobacco, Virginia's most historic and profitable crop, put Richmond and other towns back on their feet by the early 1900s. Thanks to the demand for a popular new product called cigarettes, Virginia became one of the world's largest manufacturers of tobacco goods.

Taking advantage of a large and inexpensive labor pool and other amenities, major elements of the textile industry began to flee the North and plant roots in Southside Virginia. Mass-produced furniture plants also developed in that region.

Gradually, Virginia and the rest of the South began to recover from a war that had been fought decades before. Ironically, another war raised the region to unprecedented levels of prosperity and economic growth.

With the outbreak of war in Europe in 1939, President Franklin Roosevelt pushed a buildup of the American defense industry and armed forces. The consequences for the South, particularly Virginia, were enormous.

Major shipbuilding facilities in Hampton Roads, the construction and expansion of federal facilities across the commonwealth, and the enormous growth of the federal government in Washington, much of which spilled over into Northern Virginia, transformed the one-time Confederate state.

The opening of the Pentagon in 1943 symbolized the growing importance of the federal government to the Virginia economy. Among southern states, Virginia ranked only behind Texas in the value of defense contracts, a trend that continued for decades during the Cold War.

What if the South had won the Civil War? Speculation prevails, but it is probably safe to say that the federal government would not have come to the rescue of a Confederate South in the twentieth century.

The road to recovery would have been longer and eventual prosperity less certain. We can be thankful that history turned out the way it did.

Richmond Times Dispatch, September 4, 2011

PART III

THE LIVING
AND
THE DEAD:

HEALTH AND LIFESTYLES

When I passed the mid-century point in my life, I began to notice that conversations increasingly revolved around subjects like gall bladder surgery, bad backs, prostate cancer, hip replacements, and in my case, Parkinson's disease. Note that most of those ailments are common among older people. They also have become more prevalent because people live much longer than ever.

There is a tendency to look at the past nostalgically, to the so-called "good old days." But I suspect that if we asked people if they could go back and live in an earlier time, most would answer in the negative if they became aware of what life was like before the advent of modern medicine.

It was not until the twentieth century that death was no longer a constant companion of the living. Until then, a simple paper cut could turn into a deadly infection. Epidemics swept through communities with little warning and with little under-

standing of how respond to them. Most physicians thought bad air rather than deadly microbes killed people. People did not know that basic sanitation could prevent illness.

Never in history have a people had it so good as Americans do today. Of course, there are exceptions, but most of us enjoy a degree of health, wealth, and comfort that would have been beyond the imagination of our ancestors. I hope the following essays help you realize that the "good old days" are now.

25

BIVOUACS OF THE DEAD
(MILITARY CEMETERIES)

The United States has done a remarkable job of preserving and interpreting its historic battlefields, largely through the efforts of the National Park Service and organizations like the Civil War Trust. Go to Europe, however, and you will be hard-pressed to find anything comparable, even for the most significant military clashes in history.

Reminders of previous wars, however, can be found in another form. Over the years, I have visited numerous World War I and II military cemeteries in Europe -- American, French, British and German. The look and feel of these final resting places reveal a lot about the nations they represent.

The immaculately manicured American cemeteries are noted for their stark beauty and order, with graves aligned in strict military precision as if on parade. Their pristine condition reflects a wealthy country that spent more treasure on its soldiers, both living and dead, than any other nation. Row upon row of crosses—and occasional Stars of David—carry the names of the fallen, along with home states, military units and the dates of death. Despite the existence of rigid segregation back in the States then, black and white GI's were buried together without regard to skin color. The son of Italian immigrants can lie next to a blue-blooded Ivy Leaguer, evidence that America was a melting pot nation.

British cemeteries have a certain sad poignancy about them, with individual flower plantings on graves, no doubt a reflection the nation's love of gardening. Most British military graves have modest slab markers listing the soldiers' units and their death dates. Some have a photographic image of the soldier attached to the marker. It is not unusual to find a few inscribed lines of poetry or Bibles verses on the headstones. These cemeteries represent a once-mighty British Empire, with large numbers of graves holding the remains of lads from Canada, Australia, New Zealand, South Africa or the West Indies.

While the American and British burial grounds are in some ways inspiring, French and German cemeteries are different.

The French World War I cemetery at Verdun is the eeriest place I have ever visited. The known dead are buried in standard graves, marked by crosses, Stars of David and Muslim symbols. But the bones of tens of thousands of unidentified sons of France, mingled with nameless Germans, can be seen piled high in the cemetery's somber ossuary. It struck me that even though France was on the winning side of the so-called Great War, its cost in lives was so great that the French people lacked the will to go through another similar ordeal two decades later.

German military cemeteries from World War II are dark, somber places, leaving no doubt as to who lost the war. Going from grave to grave in the cemetery at Normandy, I saw those of young men and boys from all regions of Germany. Most were members of the regular German army, the Wehrmacht, but many had served in the dreaded SS, Hitler's elite, fanatical shock troops. All are buried under Christian crosses watched over by statues of hooded figures in mourning. Unlike American, British or French World War II cemeteries, not a single grave is marked with a Star of David.

Go to a German cemetery from World War I, however, and you will find Star of David headstones with Jewish names on them scattered throughout, denoting the final resting place of Jews who fought and died for their country in large numbers. Yet within two decades, their country would turn on them. Even Jewish veterans who had served bravely in World War I were not spared from the horrors of the Holocaust. The stark contrast between German World War I and World War II cemeteries reflects that most tragic chapter in history.

Regardless of the distinctive national character of these cemeteries, they all have something in common. They are the eternal encampments of men whose lives were cut short.

John McCrae's famous poem, "In Flanders Fields," written in 1915, easily comes to mind as you gaze upon these vast bivouacs of the dead.

> In Flanders fields the poppies blow
> Between the crosses, row on row,
> That mark our place, and in the sky
> The larks, still bravely singing, fly
> Scarce hear amid the guns below
> We are the dead. Short days ago
> We lived, felt dawn, saw sunset glow,
> Loved and were loved, and now we lie
> In Flanders fields. . . .

Words from nearly two thousand years ago by Roman writer Publilus Syrus are just as relevant now as then: "As men, we are all equal in the presence of death."

Richmond Times Dispatch, November 3, 2013

26

My Fear of a Demon:
Living with Parkinson's Disease

I remember three things about Sundays in a small Southern town in the 1950s - church, Sunday dinner, and afternoon visits to relatives and friends. Those visits were an ordeal for children. Warned in advance by my parents to behave, I fidgeted and squirmed as I sat through seemingly hours of boring adult conversation.

I especially dreaded the occasional calls we made on Aunt Mamie and Uncle Sexton. My uncle was the reason, because I had never seen anyone like him. Sexton Coppinger was a perfectly nice man, but he scared me.

He spoke in barely audible whispers. He drooled. His hands were curled up like claws. His constantly writhing body and limbs frightened me the most. Some terrible demon seemed to possess him. I now know what that demon was: Parkinson's disease. It led to his death within five years.

I never dreamed something like that could happen to me. For most of my life I was blessed with excellent health. When I reached my late 50s, however, I began to notice things about myself that I dismissed as fatigue, stress, and the aging process. I had been running three miles daily, but then I couldn't quite finish that last mile. My handwriting began to look like that of an old man. My movements became overly deliberate and rigid. I slurred my words when I spoke. Expression washed away from my face. I found it difficult to concentrate at work. I knew something was wrong when people started asking me if I had been ill.

After months of hoping I would get better, I finally decided to see my doctor. He examined me thoroughly and had me perform a few simple tasks with my hands, arms, and feet. Follow-up tests revealed Parkinson's disease as the diagnosis. My wife and I were stunned. We broke down in tears, terrified at what the future held for us. Visions of Uncle Sexton haunted me. His demon had now entered my body. The possibility of giving up a job I loved and the worry that I would become an invalid plunged me into depression.

Five years later, however, I am doing remarkably well, despite the disease's subtle but steady progress. Although I retired early, I nevertheless worked full-time until recently. Many people with Parkinson's withdraw socially, but I decided to be open about it. I also determined to stay active and productive. Thanks to being a fitness fanatic prior to my diagnosis, I have found that regular exercise is more important than ever. Every day I don't work out or do something meaningful, I've lost to the Parkinson's demon.

Key to coping with the disease has been the support of my family and friends, especially a small Parkinson's support group called the "Movers and Shakers." But most effective has been access I've had to first-rate care at McGuire Veterans Hospital in Richmond.

My military service during the Vietnam War qualified me as a patient for McGuire's comprehensive Parkinson's treatment center. There I see skilled Parkinson's specialists like Dr. Vince Calabrese and Nurse Peggy Roberge. They have put me on the proper medications, a tricky business with this disease. For now my life is more or less normal, thanks to this program. I often surprise people when I tell them I have Parkinson's, although I'm sometimes rudely thrust back to reality when I'm under stress or overly tired.

Until a recent announcement from Virginia Commonwealth University, a comprehensive Parkinson's treatment center has been limited to veterans in our area. With the recruitment of Dr. James Bennett to head a team of leading experts in Parkinson's, the VCU medical college will work closely with McGuire Hospital to provide a comprehensive research and treatment center for anyone with the disease.

Physicians like Dr. Bennett have made a huge difference in the quality of life and provide hope for those of us who have incurable diseases. I think back to Uncle Sexton and now realize how fortunate I am, thanks to the many advances in medical science. My three-year-old grandson is the source of that revelation. He is not the least bit afraid of his "grandaddy," and we spend countless hours playing when we're together. I only wish that I could have known Uncle Sexton better. My mother always told me what a wonderful man he was. Sadly, I saw only the Parkinson's demon in him.

Richmond Times Dispatch, June 29, 2009

27

THE HUMAN LIFESPAN:
LIVE LONGER AND PROSPER?

A t the end of the second millennium, numerous pundits offered their opinions on the most significant developments of the past 1,000 years. Their long list mostly emphasized science and technology such as manned flight, telecommunications, quantum physics, advances in medicine, computer applications, the harnessing of electricity and atomic power.

Which of their offerings will have the greatest consequences for the present and future? My candidate is the virtual doubling of the human lifespan in the twentieth century.

Indeed, it has been only within the past hundred years that death wasn't a constant companion of humanity. At the time of Christ, the average human lifespan was only about twenty years, a figure that changed little for nineteen centuries. During George Washington's presidency, for example, the average had increased to only twenty-four years. Germs, viruses, accidents, lack of sanitation and poor diet meant that people lived short, dirty and often brutal existences, even if they survived childhood. Infant mortality rates were as high as 400 per 1,000 live births in the eighteenth century.

During the next two hundred years, however, the human lifespan increased dramatically. By the turn of the twentieth century, it was double that of Washington's time, and now, it has nearly doubled again. This was no accident. Acceptance of the germ theory was followed by improved personal hygiene and sanitation methods that saw widespread gains in the nineteenth century. Advances in the practice of medicine enabled physicians to treat ailments with a greater degree of sophistication than ever before. Pharmaceuticals once based heavily on folk remedies and the imagination of their makers became strictly regulated by government authority and more effective in their application to patients.

The growth of a strong public health system was equally important. Modern and well-equipped hospitals, staffed by highly trained physicians and nurses, sprang up in most developed nations. Significant funding from government and private sources for medical research has led to cures and improved treatment of numerous diseases. Mass inoculations for polio, mumps, measles, smallpox and influenza have spared untold numbers of lives. The infant mortality rate has dropped to only about seven per 1,000 live births.

These advances, along with improvements in diet and increased emphasis on healthy living, have resulted in plunging death rates in developed countries, helping lead to a population explosion. The world's population, for example, required only 40 years after 1950 to double from 2.5 billion to 5 billion. It exceeded 6 billion by 2000, and at the current rate it may reach 12 billion by this century's end. The demand on Earth's resources such as water, food, fuel, soil and clean air is tremendous and grows with each new person born. The evidence mounts that climate change is tied to population growth.

History reveals sudden and dramatic decreases in population. Archaeologists now argue that the Western Hemisphere's population on the eve of Columbus' first voyage to the "New World" was about 100 million. Yet a century later, nearly ninety percent of that number had been wiped out, victims of germs and viruses introduced by Europeans. For centuries, epidemics ravaged various parts of the world, killing millions. Deaths from the world wars of the twentieth century numbered some 80 million. As horrific as those numbers are, they produced only temporary and slight disturbances to the upward trend in population.

What, then, does the future hold for us and our offspring? Will the average human lifespan double again as it did in the past century? Will the world's rapid population growth continue and are there sufficient resources to sustain it? Can it be slowed? If not, how will we cope?

There are no simple solutions. Education and awareness are perhaps the best approaches, but our elected officials seem squeamish when it comes to discussing hot-button issues such as sex education, family planning and the use of contraceptives. It was not an issue in this year's presidential campaign. Leaders in developing countries, where birth rates and poverty are high and literacy is low, also ignore the subject.

Tax concessions favoring families with fewer children and penalties for too many have been advocated. Authoritarian China introduced its "One Child" policy in the 1970s, penalizing parents who produced more than one baby. The Chinese birthrate has slowed, but few other countries are willing to embrace such a drastic measure.

Overpopulation is a topic that cannot be ignored if our children and grandchildren are to have a quality of life more like ours than our ancestors'. The words of the late essayist Edward Abbey apply: "A crowded society is a restrictive society; an overcrowded society becomes an authoritarian, repressive, and murderous society." The time has come to wake up about one of the most pressing issues of our time.

Richmond Times Dispatch, December 16, 2012

28

DELEGATING DEATH AND DYING IN AMERICA

Death was humanity's constant companion for most of recorded history. If we average total births and deaths only 200 years ago, the lifespan of an American was about twenty-five years. People died of any number of causes. As late as 1918, epidemics periodically swept through the world's population, killing people by the millions. Without lifesaving equipment, modern pharmaceuticals, or well-trained physicians to tend to patients, long, lingering deaths were unusual. Healthcare costs were a fraction of what they are now, even in today's dollars.

Surrounded by death, people tended to be fatalistic. One man living in eighteenth-century Virginia recalled that "by the time I was ten, I looked upon life as fleeting and there was little need to dwell on melancholy things."

Handling death was up close and personal. People mostly died at home, where their remains were prepared by their loved ones for burial in nearby family plots or churchyards. Soon-to-decompose bodies were hurried into the ground, most wrapped in shrouds. Until the nineteenth century, only the well-to-do were buried in coffins or afforded grave markers. Slaves were often interred in unmarked plots segregated from white graves. Although the average human lifespan remained relatively short until the twentieth century, the way Americans handled death changed. As the nation became increasingly prosperous in the 1800's, Americans began to adopt British and French customs, including formal mourning and where the dead were buried. With church graveyards and small public burial grounds becoming overcrowded in fast growing American cities, the creation of large park-like cemeteries such as Richmond's Hollywood grew into a movement.

The haste to bury slowed as Americans became more concerned with preserving the remains. Embalming was introduced from Europe in the mid-nineteenth century, a practice that gained momentum during the Civil War when more people chose to have their loved ones embalmed. A turning point in public awareness of the process was the cross country journey of Abraham Lincoln's body after his assassination. Newspapers reported how well preserved he was, and soon embalming became standard practice.

With significant advances in medical science, improved nutrition, and people leading healthier lifestyles in the twentieth century, the average human lifespan reached the mid-70's. Dying and death in America fundamentally changed. We Americans evolved into a death denying and death defying society. Unlike previous generations who accepted death as a given, death became the enemy to be beaten at all costs. Doctors and their patients came to believe that a patient's death was a failure to practice proper medicine. The process of dying slowed.

Patients diagnosed with terminal illnesses could live for years thanks to great advances in medical science. People who are declared "brain dead" can now be kept alive for years, hooked up to life-sustaining equipment. Advances in organ transplant surgery, valve replacements, and many other procedures once considered as miracles are now regarded as routine and have extended the lives of millions of people.

But as people lived longer, age-related diseases such as Alzheimer's and osteoporosis have emerged and often have led to long, slow exits from life. The cost of medical care soared to astronomical heights—about one-fourth of medical treatment occurs in the last year of life (especially with intensive care). With the view that death should be put off for as long as possible, many doctors began to blur the line between saving lives and preventing death. Patients increasingly grasped for any straw of hope, fighting when they should probably surrender. By dying long, sometime undignified deaths for themselves, a patient's loved ones began to experience an agonizing ordeal of waiting.

In addition, death was taken outside of the home and into hospitals, nursing homes, and assisted living facilities for most

Americans. Since the earliest days of Colonial America, the elderly were cared for at home. It was common to have three generations living under one roof as senior parents settled in with their adult children. But in the late twentieth century, many of America's elderly moved or were moved into communities and facilities that specialized in people of their own age group. This separation of the elderly from their children and grandchildren further removed people from the process of death.

In 1900, approximately eighty-five percent of people died at home, but by the 1990's, the numbers were nearly reversed. Why the shift? If anything it is tied to growth in American prosperity. By the mid-twentieth century, Americans were the world's wealthiest people. With prosperity came the delegation of the unpleasant things in life such as waste disposal, slaughtering animals for food, and preparing the dead for burial. A prosperous people could pay others to do these onerous tasks, and in the twentieth century, a whole new industry, funeral homes, spread throughout the country. What is the future of death in America? Although the Hospice movement is bringing more people home to die, most of us will end life elsewhere. With a growing public belief that the body is a temporal container, cremations are expected to exceed burials in a matter of years. Projections are that healthcare will become even more expensive as people live longer.

Despite all of the advances in medicine, the end will inevitably come to us all. Our control of life and death still is limited. The words of Socrates are as relevant today as they were two thousand years ago: "No one knows whether death may not be the greatest of all blessings . . . yet men fear it as if they knew it as the greatest of evils."

Richmond Times Dispatch, January 31, 2015

29

THE GREAT FLU PANDEMIC OF 1918-19

As we enter the heart of flu season, I am reminded that baby boomers like me are only one generation removed from a deadly and virulent virus that swept the world, killing tens of millions of people.

For those who survived, the Great Influenza Pandemic of 1918-19 was seared in their memories. My family elders told me compelling stories about that dreadful time. No matter where they lived, country or city, there was no escape from the deadly virus.

One of my mother's most vivid childhood memories was of lying in bed with excruciating pain wracking her body and gasping for air with every breath. She obviously survived, but her beloved aunt died at age twenty-six only two days after becoming ill.

Her premature death was not unusual. Unlike today's flu that strikes the elderly hardest, half of the deaths from the 1918 pandemic were people between the ages of twenty and forty. Fewer than one percent were over sixty-five. It struck viciously and quickly. A perfectly healthy person could die within two or three days. Another unusual feature of the pandemic was its peak in the summer and fall rather than in winter.

Where and why the first outbreak occurred is subject to debate. Many experts argue that the virus jumped from pigs to humans, and its first significant outbreak occurred in March 1918 at Fort Riley, Kansas, where thousands of soldiers were in training for the fighting in Europe. As they were shipped out in large numbers, doughboys carried the virus with them, spreading it to civilians on the East Coast and then Europe. Within months it jumped to Asia, Africa and South America.

Given the flu's killing power and rapid spread, physicians and public health officials were taken aback. In the two decades leading up to 1918, great advances had been made in medical science, including acceptance of the germ theory; the development of inoculations and more effective pharmaceuticals; and increased emphasis on sanitation and hygiene.

Some medical experts argued that epidemics were at an end. The new flu, however, proved them wrong. Modern medicine at first seemed helpless in the face of such a deadly enemy.

Virginia's response to the crisis was typical. In September 1918, several sailors in Norfolk were diagnosed with Spanish flu. A month later some 200,000 cases were reported in the Commonwealth. Overwhelmed by the numbers, doctors treated patients the best way they could, some resorting to less-than-effective methods.

Doctors, nevertheless, understood that flu was spread from person to person, and were able to persuade public officials to ban large gatherings and issue face masks to the public.

Authorities closed the State Fair in October. Richmond city officials banned public gatherings, including weddings, movies, plays and other events for several weeks. Churches suspended services. Schools were closed, and some like John Marshall High School, were turned into emergency hospitals.

Across the country, the illness subsided briefly as winter set in, only to break out again. The pandemic occurred in three waves. The first struck in the spring and summer of 1918, the second and most severe in the fall, and a final wave in the spring of 1919.

Gradually, quarantines and restrictions on public gatherings were lifted. People began to adjust to a return to peace with the end of World War I and the end of the dreaded illness.

By the summer of 1919, Spanish flu disappeared as quickly and mysteriously as it broke out, never to return. In all, nearly 675,000 Americans had succumbed to the deadly virus. Globally, as many as 50 million people died, more than were lost in World War I. The flu, however, lingered in other ways, particularly its impact on the economy.

Life insurance claims soared, driving many companies out of business. Small businesses that had been forced to shut down during the pandemic or lost workers to death often went bankrupt. This, combined with the disruptions caused by the transition to a peacetime economy, led to a major post-war recession.

Will the world be revisited by such a deadly killer? Most scientists say that it is possible, especially if a treatment-resistant "super flu" were to evolve. Even with our ability to detect and treat disease and communicate rapidly, our globalized society, combined with modern transportation systems, means that an outbreak could spread rapidly around the globe. Increased population densities would exacerbate the problem.

Medical science can offer solutions to prevent another pandemic. We live in a time, however, when the political process is extremely partisan and fractious, making problem-solving difficult. Would that lack of unity prevent us from effectively defending ourselves against such a threat? I wonder.

Richmond Times Dispatch, January 13, 2013

30

HELPING HOMELESS VETERANS

Lately I've been seeing more beggars standing at street corners in Richmond. Like many motorists, I feel uncomfortable when I stop at a red light near a bedraggled person holding a crude sign pleading for money or food.

I avoid eye contact, but my uneasiness increases with every second that I sit there. I am not afraid of this hapless person; rather I feel guilty. But as soon as the light turns green, I hit the accelerator feeling temporarily remorseful for not handing him some change. On the other hand, I also feel guilty when I do relent and give money to a beggar. I wonder if I am only enabling him to sink lower into a world of drug or alcohol abuse.

When I was at McGuire Veterans Hospital recently, I picked up some discouraging information that has made me think about what to do with some beggars. Approximately one third of homeless people (mostly men) are veterans, although they make up only eleven percent of the American population. On any given night, nearly 300,000 people who have served their country in the military are living on the street. The number of homeless Vietnam-era veterans is greater than the number who died in that war.

Many of the poor souls wandering the streets never have recovered from the physical and psychological wounds they sustained in war. Large numbers have substance abuse problems that keep them unemployed. Some warriors who have come back from Iraq and Afghanistan have had trouble adjusting to civilian life in part because such a small percentage of the American population now has ever served in the armed forces, much less experienced combat. This has created a gulf between cultures that leaves many veterans estranged.

Our country has a long history of assisting its veterans. Following the American Revolution, Congress provided land in the western territories for those who had served. After subsequent conflicts, veterans received pensions, bonuses, medical care and financial support for education. Since its founding in 1930, the U.S. Veterans Administration (now the Department of Veteran Affairs) has developed the world's most comprehensive system of assistance for former service members.

The V.A., however, faces one of the greatest challenges in its history. The system is over-extended by soaring demands as Vietnam-era veterans age and require increased medical care.

If that isn't enough, American military involvement in the Middle East and Asia over the past decade is placing additional pressure on the system. Combine those factors with the threat of federal budget cuts, and we can speculate on what will happen to veterans who might no longer receive medical attention. Many probably will show up on our streets asking for handouts. What can we do to help them?

The best way is to give your time and talent. Visit the Veterans Affairs website (www.va.gov) and find out how you can volunteer at your local V.A. hospital or assist veterans in other ways. Donate small items such as toiletries, coffee, cookies, new or used clothing in good condition, and phone cards to the V.A. hospital.

What about homeless veterans who don't avail themselves of the V.A.? I have spent much of my professional career asking people for money during numerous fundraising efforts. I learned over the years that most sophisticated donors know there are limits to what they can do, so they target their philanthropy. They only give to certain causes or within specific parameters such as medical research, arts and culture, or higher education.

I have adopted a similar protocol when responding to people wanting handouts. I don't initiate contact with beggars, but if I'm approached by one, I ask him if he is a veteran. If he answers yes, I query him about his branch of service -- Army, Navy, Air Force, Marine Corps, or Coast Guard. Then I try to learn more by asking him about what he did in service -- his MOS (military occupational specialty).

If he seems clueless in answering my question, I tell him that I only give to veterans. But if he says something like "Eleven Bravo" (11B), which stands for an Army infantry rifleman, or 0312, a Marine armored vehicle crewman, I know that he has served. I used to give a dollar or two, but I've started carrying a few $5 gift certificates from McDonald's and Subway in my wallet and car. Now I thank him for his service, hand him a certificate, and encourage him to get back on his feet.

When I was an Army officer, we were trained to "take care of our troops first." Call me naïve or self-serving, but if my modest gesture helps some beggar veterans even in a small way, my sense of guilt is eased knowing that I am taking care of the troops.

Richmond Times Dispatch, September 22, 2013

.

MEMORY

ONE AND ONE HALF MILLION

ES OF THE CONFEDERA

AM ES O

Courtesy of the Virginia Historical Society.
Photo by Meg M. Eastman

PART IV

EDUCATION,
MUSEUMS
AND THE
CRAFT OF HISTORY

History holds a paradoxical place in the United States today. On the one hand, some pundits contend that Americans are woefully ignorant of their history. On the other, evidence suggests that the state of history in America has never been better. There are more museums and other organizations devoted to history in the United States, both in total number and per capita, than any other country in the world. Old neighborhoods containing numerous architectural gems were once razed without anyone batting an eye. The hallowed grounds of Civil War battlefields once lost to shopping malls, sprawling suburbs, and superhighways are now protected by law and preservation organizations as never before.

Free and open societies value history and the lessons it has to impart. They devote significant resources to its preservation and dissemination. Totalitarian societies on the other hand have manipulated, denied public access to, and even destroyed the evidence of the past. It is if they are afraid of what history has to teach. I am thankful not only that I could devote my career to history, but also live in a country that allows me to investigate and write about the past freely and openly without fear of censorship.

31

A Comprehensive Museum: Stroll Through Virginia's Rich History

S
ome years ago when I lived in Nashville, I accompanied my daughter's third-grade class to the newly opened Tennessee State Museum. By walking through nearly 50,000 square feet of galleries, we saw hundreds of remarkable artifacts, from prehistoric stone implements to modern gadgets representing the atomic age. Although I had studied Tennessee history for years, the visit to the museum gave me a journey through time that I could not have experienced otherwise. Since its opening in the early 1950s, this museum has offered a unique examination of the state's history to hundreds of thousands of visitors every year.

Is this museum in Tennessee unusual? Not really. In the last two decades, most states have spent millions of dollars for museums to collect and exhibit the artifacts that tell their people's story. From Washington state to Florida, from Maine to Arizona, a traveler can learn the story of virtually every state in the Union by visiting their state history museums. Our neighbors to the South are flocking in large numbers to a grand new museum in Raleigh that covers four centuries of North Carolina history. The Commonwealth of Kentucky, the stepchild of Virginia, recently appropriated several million dollars for the Kentucky Historical Society to build a new state history center and museum.

Where can Virginians go to gain a thorough understanding of the Commonwealth's past? Without question, the Old Dominion has a history that few states can match and some of the finest history museums in the country. From Colonial Williamsburg to Monticello to the Valentine Museum, specific aspects and periods of Virginia history are interpreted very effectively.

This approach to learning the full scope of Virginia's past, however, tends to be episodic and scattered. We must travel to several museums to learn about colonial times, to historic houses to put important families and early leaders into any meaningful context, to many battlefields and the Museum of the Confederacy to understand the ebb and flow of events of the Civil War, or to a host of local museums to learn about a particular community's past. With few exceptions, the period after Appomattox is overlooked entirely.

A top priority in the recent expansion of the Virginia Historical Society has been to create a "Museum of Virginia History" that provides the only comprehensive interpretation of that subject to be found in the Commonwealth. Thanks to a generous gift from Philip Morris, the centerpiece will be a permanent exhibit allowing the visitor to walk through more than four centuries of Virginia history. A panel of distinguished scholars is helping us plan our story line and select objects from our large collection of Virginiana to be included in the exhibit, scheduled to open in late 1995.

In addition to the permanent exhibit, our museum offers changing exhibitions on subjects that affected all Virginians. Two years ago, we explored the healing arts before the advent of modern medicine, and showed the early blending in Virginia of three medical cultures -- European, African, and Native American. Last year, we opened "V for Virginia," a powerful exhibit that demonstrated how World War II permanently changed the Commonwealth and its people. Smaller versions of both exhibits have traveled to cities throughout the state, as will most of our special changing exhibitions, pending funding.

Future exhibits will deal with Virginia's role in the exploration and peopling of the American West, the civil rights movement, its Native American heritage, and the history of crime and punishment. As always, our exhibits are accompanied by workshops for teachers and special tours for school groups.

How much do our Museum and related educational programs cost in tax dollars? Not a cent. Because of Virginia's economic difficulties, we lost our small state appropriation two years ago. Ironically, because of Virginia's tax code relating to not-for-profit institutions, we pay the state nearly $25,000 a year in sales tax.

Thanks to the generosity of hundreds of individuals, corporations, and foundations, the Historical Society has raised nearly $12 million to create new museum galleries, a beautiful new research library, and modern storage for our collections, and to develop educational programs throughout the state.

Our work is far from over, but our gratitude is profound to those who have given so munificently to the Historical Society. Their generosity has allowed us to make an important gift to the people of Virginia, one we hope to continue year after year. As the Commonwealth enters its fifth century, its people deserve no less. In the meantime, we hope they will come and learn from the new Museum of Virginia History we are creating.

Richmond Times Dispatch, November 23, 1992

32

AMERICANS DO EMBRACE THEIR HISTORY

I n recent years several influential commentators have argued that we face a crisis of historical amnesia in America. Lynne Cheney declared that "a refusal to remember the past is a primary characteristic of our nation." Pulitzer Prize-winning historian David McCullough warned that "we, in our time, are raising a new generation of Americans, who, to an alarming degree, are historically illiterate." Louis Harlan, former president of the American Historical Association, lamented that "the present public ignorance of our cultural heritage . . . has alarming implications for the future of our nation." This perceived crisis has been a strong rallying cry for reforms in the American education system and the teaching of history. It has been used as evidence to cite what is wrong with this country.

I confess that until a few years ago, I held many of the same sentiments, and at times I still decry the misuse and misunderstanding of history. But I have become more sanguine about the state of history in our country. Most of the arguments about historical ignorance are that it is a growing problem and that the American public is becoming less well-grounded in its knowledge of the past. Of course, this assumes that previous generations were much more knowledgeable about history. That it was taught better in schools. That textbooks were more interesting and meaningful. That historical information was easily available to the public. That most Americans were fonts of information about the past.

Could this be the case, however, when only 50 years ago, more than 40 percent of the population did not have high-school degrees? Can we say that Americans once had a "better" understanding of history when many of its important aspects were all but ignored in textbooks and classrooms? Was it really taught that much better in previous generations? I, like many of my contemporaries in the '50s and '60s, was "taught" history by a football coach, who seemed more interested in next week's game than in the Louisiana Purchase.

History occupies a paradoxical and problematic place in contemporary American culture. On the one hand, it is widely believed that we face a crisis of historical amnesia. In other words, the glass is half-empty. But is it possible that the glass is half-full - that the American people value and support history to a far greater degree than is commonly thought? Indeed, there is a flip side to the so-called history crisis, and there is strong evidence of an enormous interest in the past.

Take, for example, the proliferation of museums and historical societies, resulting in record museum attendance and a growing historically oriented tourism market. Since the American Bicentennial in 1976, the number of history museums in this country has more than doubled, reflecting the willingness of the public to invest huge sums of money and effort in preserving the past. As a member of the accreditation team of the American Association of Museums, I have observed the phenomenon of new local and regional museums all over the country, from Virginia to Kansas to California.

According to a recent survey, nearly 40 percent of all museums in the world are now located in the United States. Most do an excellent job, thanks to a strong emphasis on scholarship and a willingness to deal with subjects that once were regarded as too controversial. So if we look only at the proliferation of museums, there is reason to be less pessimistic about the state of history. But museums aren't the only reason to consider the glass half-full.

History is prevalent in the media. Although much of television still can be considered a vast wasteland, there is more good history in that medium reaching a bigger audience than ever before. For the past several years *The American Experience* on PBS has presented a variety of important subjects on our nation's history, done with sensitivity and based on solid scholarship. A whole network is devoted to history, and good history can be found on other networks, including the commercial stations.

Even though he has been the subject of criticism, Ken Burns has presented several historical documentaries that have stimulated remarkable public interest. The ratings for his series on the Civil War were the highest in PBS history and rivaled those of the major commercial networks. In the following two years, sales of Civil War books soared, as did visitation to museums and battle-fields. His other series on Thomas Jefferson, Lewis and Clark, baseball, and jazz have had similar though less profound results.

With the advent of the worldwide web, it is estimated that there are at least 10,000 websites in the United States alone devoted to history. Through this development, history now is accessible to people almost anywhere in the world.

We have invested heavily in our website at the Virginia Historical Society, and it is having a profound effect on our institution. Our card catalogue is online now, making detailed information on our collections available to anyone on the face of the globe with access to the web. In addition, our site enables us to offer virtual tours of exhibits, send lesson plans to teachers, and even sell books from our museum shop. Use of our website has soared, and the number of visits we received last year approached a quarter of a million. Multiply those hits by the total number of history websites and you realize there are a lot of people who are learning from a whole new source.

There are other signs that the glass is half-full. Thanks to the growth of the historic preservation movement and related legislation in the past 25 years, historic structures and neighborhoods have a degree of protection that did not exist in the past. Because of tax credits, we are seeing huge investments of money in adaptive re-use of historic buildings and in urban renewal. Genealogy is one of the fastest growing pastimes in America. Once the domain of people seeking admission to patriotic societies, genealogy in the past several years has become much more democratic (small "d"), with people of all ethnic and socio-economic backgrounds seeking information on their roots. A glance at almost any non-fiction best-seller list will usually reveal a strong presence of history books such as David McCullough's *John Adams* or any of Stephen Ambrose's works. The number of students enrolled in college history courses has rebounded from the declines of previous decades.

I could cite other examples of why I am more upbeat about the state of history in this country, but I do have concerns. I am bothered by the misuse of history to justify political arguments or personal ends. I am not a regular listener to radio talk shows, but I was appalled by what I heard from announcers and listeners alike over the controversy relating to the Confederate flag in recent years.

Although there have been some fine movies based on history, too often we see Hollywood's manipulation of the past in the name of artistic freedom. From Oliver Stone's conspiracy-laced interpretations to the big screen spectacle *The Patriot*, films often are filled with egregious errors and gross distortions of the past.

I am concerned that scores on the history section of standardized testing in schools are usually low, but I suspect they would have been no higher in my high-school days.

Despite these concerns, I am not convinced our country is losing its national memory. I have visited museums and historic sites in countries around the world. In so many places, the records and evidence of the past were at one time or another systematically destroyed. We saw a chilling example of that in Afghanistan even before the current international crisis. Over the past few years, members of the Taliban began to obliterate historic Buddhist icons and empty the shelves of the national museum and archives in Kabul. As one Taliban official declared: "There is no place for sentimental feelings with these old things."

Although our record is not spotless, history has done well in this country. We may not like certain aspects of our past, and we may not agree on how it is interpreted, but we're not afraid of it. We turn to our past for instruction, especially in the aftermath of September 11. Rarely have the news media called so much upon the expertise of historians as they have in the current crisis. Indeed, this is a time when we who value and preserve the history of our country hold a special place and purpose.

In good times and bad, history - whether in museums, on television, or in books - is a prime source for putting the events of today in perspective. It imparts a sense of time, place, and stability. It provides an opportunity for dialogue, debate, and the exchange of ideas. It protects the collective memory of our people and reminds us that together we are strong. It reminds us that there is comfort in the past. As David McCullough observes: "History is an aid to navigation in perilous times."

Despite alarms to the contrary, the American people do value their history. We are not afraid of our past as some other societies are, and we have done a remarkably good job of preserving it and making it available to a wide public. We learn from it. As such, history is a key component of this country's remarkable experiment in self-government and a bedrock of our democracy.

Richmond Times Dispatch, February 3, 2002

33

MUSEUMS COMPETE WITH CABLE, SPORTS, MOVIES, MALLS FOR VISITORS

A t long last the economy seems to be turning around after three tough years. For those of us who run museums, the news is especially welcome. We have become almost used to the grim litany of reports of hard times coming from our colleagues around the country.

While we hope that things will begin to look up with an improving economy, a troublesome phenomenon remains; in recent years most American museums have reported declining, or at best flat, visitation numbers. Some observers have blamed this drop on the aftermath of 9/11, the downturn in the economy, and high gasoline prices. It is natural to hope that museum attendance will rebound. But will it? Without question, the events of the past few years have had an effect, but the trend toward declining visitation actually began before 9/11 and the sour economy.

Colonial Williamsburg, a bellwether museum for the nation, saw its numbers go flat, then downward in the booming '90s. Last year that great museum experienced its lowest attendance in decades. Although school-group tours continue to pour in during the academic year, general museum visitation at the Virginia Historical Society has plateaued, as it has for most other museums in the region. Many newly opened museums around the country that had projected high attendance have fallen far short of their goals and have had to scale back their operations. Some are barely hanging on. A few have closed their doors.

Why has this happened, especially with history museums? There is the temptation to blame it on a "growing" problem of historical apathy or historical amnesia in this country. But, as I have written in this newspaper before, there is plenty of evidence that Americans do embrace their history. Never has history been more available and accessible to so many people than now. For one, there has been a remarkable proliferation of history museums over the past quarter of a century. According to several estimates, the number has doubled.

The great expansion of cable television channels has made history available seven days a week, 24 hours a day. With the advent of the internet, it is estimated that there are at least 10,000 websites in the United States devoted solely to history.

Gone are the days when access to the past was limited. Now there is a plethora of ways to learn about and enjoy history. But is it possible that with so many options available to the public, most museums can no longer expect a rising visitation curve? Some observers wonder frankly if there are too many museums to sustain adequately. They also surmise that the audience for history becomes ever more diluted with the opening of each new museum.

Of course, the competition for visitors is not limited to other history options. Never before have there been so many ways to fill our free time. Psychologist Barry Schwartz observes in his most recent book, *The Paradox of Choice: Why More is Less*, that Americans are bombarded with choices allowing people to flit from one activity to another.

How does this relate to museums? In addition to many other history venues and an abundance of other cultural attractions, museums now compete with the proliferation of sports in America, from year-round youth soccer leagues to ESPN 24 hours a day. They compete with multiplex movie theaters that can offer new feature films far faster than new museum exhibitions can be produced. They contend with theme parks that are within driving distance of most homes in America. They vie with shopping malls. It may be no coincidence that the parking lots at Stony Point and Short Pump are full much of the time, while those of area museums have space available.

What does all of this portend for history museums? For one, wise museum management will carefully assess visitation projections and craft financial forecasts accordingly. Too many museums have gotten themselves in trouble with pie-in-the-sky projections. Museums that are heavily dependent on gate receipts should develop strategies for diversifying their revenue and work on creating or strengthening endowments. They should consistently measure their performance, seeking reliable feedback from the public they serve as they plan for the future.

Despite the current problems with traditional visitation there is hope for the future. For example, while the numbers through the door are flat at the Virginia Historical Society, visits on our website have soared. We anticipate more than a million "virtual visits" this year. That number will increase as we add more historical information to the site. Indeed, museums are having to develop new ways to tap into the potential presented by a growing number of people who visit the past in a whole new way.

Also, several studies have shown that as people grow older their interest in history tends to increase. Lectures and other programs at the Virginia Historical Society now have overflow audiences comprised of intellectually curious seniors. To a large extent the new education wing we are building is in response to that growing demand. Indeed, lifelong learning is becoming an increasingly important responsiblity of museums.

Finally, with the impending retirement of the Baby Boom generation, history museums might see rising visitation again from people who still yearn for the unique experience of seeing "the real thing" in galleries. Museums will continue to be the stewards of the priceless treasures of our national heritage. Whatever the case, the choices consumers of history face will only increase, and those of us in the "history business" need to refine our programs and services to keep abreast of the public's evolving interests and to adapt to a changing museum paradigm.

Richmond Times Dispatch, December 19, 2004

34

TEACHING HISTORY WITH ALL
ITS WARTS

Recent news coming out of Oklahoma about the teaching of American history made me think of one of the most remarkable letters I have ever received. It came to me in April 1985 when I was serving as the executive director of the East Tennessee Historical Society in Knoxville. It was posted from Lublin, Poland, six years before the collapse of the Soviet Union.

The handwritten letter's author was Andrew Pieczonka, a university student who had found the address of the historical society in an old directory. He wrote:

> "[I am} interested in everything that is connected with your wonderful country. In my opinion the U.S.A. is one of the seven wonders of the present-day world. Your country is my ideal. It is the symbol of Democracy and Freedom. To know the history of the U.S.A. well is the greatest and most important aim of my life. Unfortunately here where I live, it is impossible to buy any books about the history of the U.S.A. Polish bookshops are full of books about the history of Russia, Germany, etc., but unfortunately there are not any books about the history of the U.S.A. even in my University Library, the amount of such books is so small that all students must fight with one another in order to read them. Sometimes I feel as if I were in an empty cage without a way out."

He then asked if we could send him any American history books, even old or damaged ones. "It is beyond expression how great my happiness would be, how thankful to you I would be if You sent me these wonderful books," he exclaimed. He closed the letter using the word "very" 300 times: "Thank you very . . . .[repeated 300 times] . . . much."

We didn't quite know what to think of the letter other than it was genuine and we wanted to respond. I called Senator Howard Baker's office for advice on the best way to fulfill the request. His foreign relations staffer told us to go ahead and send books with a note that would not be considered subversive or inflammatory. He speculated that there was a distinct possibility our package would not get through Polish security.

Following this advice, we sent Pieczonka a dozen or so books and pamphlets on United States history, including college textbooks, books on Tennessee, and one on America's presidents. After five months with no word from Poland, we assumed they had been confiscated or stolen by authorities.

Then in mid-October, a letter arrived from our man in Poland. This time he began his letter by filling ten pages with the word "very," saying , "I would like to thank You very, very, very [ten more pages] very much for the wonderful books I have received from You. I find it difficult to express to you how happy I am. I feel like dancing and jumping with joy. These are the best, most wonderful and interesting books I have ever seen. I have decided to spend all my life studying the history of the USA. This is because the history of the USA is to me the only symbol of Freedom and Democracy. LONG LIVE THE USA!"

Fast-forward twenty-five years to when I was serving as president of the Virginia Historical Society. I learned that a scholar from Poland, who was a specialist in American history, was doing research in our library. Later that day, I introduced myself to her, and after chatting with her a few minutes, I casually mentioned my letters from Andrew Pieczonka. She looked at me with astonishment, and said that he had been a student hers and that he was teaching high school history somewhere in Poland. Although she had lost touch with him, she remembered his talking about the books he had received from Tennessee. It was one of the most gratifying "small world" stories of my life.

That brings me back to what is going on in Oklahoma and other parts of the country.   Recently a committee of the Oklahoma legislature advanced a bill to ban state funds for use in teaching the advanced placement United States history course in public high schools because the course framework emphasizes, "what is bad about America" and downplays "American exceptionalism."

Similar challenges have appeared in a variety of states, including North Carolina, Texas, South Carolina, Georgia, and Colorado, where advocates have called for more "pro American" history in the classroom.   Many of the critics of the current course contend that the teaching of history should encourage patriotism, not critical thinking.   Commentators on Fox News have questioned whether students should learn that the United States is uniquely virtuous instead of flawed like any other nation.

At times the argument has gotten downright silly. Presidential contender Ben Carson declared, "Most people when they finish that course would be ready to go sign up for ISIS."

I worry when I hear these arguments about sanitizing history. If you study totalitarian regimes throughout history, you see a fear of the past. It happened in Maoist China, Nazi Germany, North Korea, the Soviet Union, and, yes, in Poland until the end of the Cold War.

It was as if their leaders were afraid of history because it might undermine the legitimacy of their regimes. The "official histories" they presented were censored and manipulated heavily. They limited people's access to the past, and denied them the ability to learn from history, warts and all.

Free and open societies, on the other hand, value history and turn to it for instruction. They do this despite what the evidence reveals. They allow free and open debate and critical thinking on how the past is perceived and interpreted.

That was something that Andrew Pieczonka desperately yearned for in 1985.

First time published.

35

HISTORY BEGINS AT HOME, NOT IN SCHOOL

In recent years, many observers have lamented the poor state of history in America, particularly among young people. Blame for lack of interest in the subject is often directed at our schools. Indeed, the teaching of history is being squeezed gradually out of the curriculum in many states.

Our schools, however, should not bear full responsibility. In many ways history is taught better today than when I was in school. In my student days, several important aspects of history were all but ignored. As it was for many young people then, history classes were a dreary recitation of dates and facts, in my case taught by our football coach.

My love of history blossomed not at school but at home. When I was eight years old, my father died suddenly from a heart attack. My mother moved our family back to a small Tennessee town, where we lived with my grandfather.

Almost from the beginning, he told me stories about the past and our family. He told me about Yankee soldiers riding up to his father's home and taking the family's livestock one winter during the Civil War. A week later a Confederate patrol came to the farm and took almost the entire remaining foodstuff. My great-grandfather and his brothers spent the rest of the winter hunting game to keep the family fed.

He also told me about those dreadful last few days of 1862 when nearly 25,000 men fell at the battle of Murfreesboro. The family could hear the rumble of cannon in the distance for three days, knowing full well that loved ones might be dying.

My mother was a storyteller too. She was a Latin teacher, and her classes were more a course in ancient history. At home, she told tales of our family that had been passed on to her.

I learned that my great-great-great grandfather from Virginia had fought in the Continental Line with Washington. She told me about the deadly flu epidemic of 1918, of how she survived but lost her beloved Aunt Stella. Of being a terrified girl when the first airplane she had ever seen flew low over the family farm.

Because of these tales, the past had captured my imagination. It excited and awed me, and it was true. It told me the story of my family: who we were and where we came from. I did not realize it then, but it connected me in time and place to the world in which I was growing up. Those stories also gave me a process -- the act of imagining the past.

I was fortunate as a child to grow up in a home where the past was made to come alive by one of the oldest ways of relating history -- storytelling. I do wonder, however, if young people today have the benefit of parents and grandparents who tell stories about the past and their families.

I have no proof of this other than personal observation, but I suspect that family storytelling has become a thing of the past, a victim of our modern lifestyle. We are all so busy.

Young people are heavily programmed in their activities today, both in school and out. Personal time with family gets crowded out of the schedule, as exemplified in one of last year's hottest documentary films, *Waiting for Superman*. Sadly, I am afraid that many children have little idea of where they came from and who they are.

Perhaps we have delegated too much responsibility to our schools when it comes to history. We should strive to bring history back home with our own children and grandchildren. I have already begun telling stories to my grandsons. These are not stories about the Civil War but about a time when I was a boy and swam in the creek in the summer; about being scared when I watched Sputnik streak across a cold winter sky; about the black man who made molasses using a mule-driven press; about riding in cars without seat belts; and about their great-grandfathers, one a genuine war hero, the other a brilliant musician who died too soon. One of these days, I will put these and other stories in writing for them.

The Roman orator Cicero observed: "To know nothing of what happened before you were born is to remain forever a child." We owe it to young people to give them a sense of the past that no classroom, textbook or standards of learning examination can.

Richmond Times Dispatch, April 10, 2011

36

THE TEST: KNOW MUCH ABOUT RICHMOND HISTORY?

I n his classic rock 'n' roll song "Wonderful World," Sam Cooke crooned, "Don't know much about history." Those words could easily apply to most Americans. It seems that every few years another study reveals our citizens are woefully ignorant of the past.

This concern is not new. An article in the Richmond *Whig* in 1846 opined that a "melancholy and ludicrous ignorance of our history prevails among our people." Education officials in Texas became alarmed when more than half of the state's high school seniors flunked a standardized history test in 1919.

Nevertheless, numerous studies reveal that most Americans have some knowledge of our national history. Whether then or now, however, they are especially ignorant of local history—the story of their own community's past. Some Scandinavian students learn their local history first, a practice not followed here.

Few American cities have a history as long and storied as Richmond's. Yet I suspect that most of its residents know little about it.

How about you? Take the following quiz to determine your knowledge of Richmond's history. Good luck!

1.   Richmond is reputed to have had the largest of which one of the following in the Western Hemisphere during the Civil War?

    a.   iron manufacturing plant
    b.   hospital

c.   textile plant
d.   rail yard
e.   none of the above

* * * * *

2.   True or false. Richmond was the third largest city in the South on the eve of the Civil War.

* * * * *

3.   When British troops captured Richmond in 1781, who among the following was governor of Virginia and was forced to flee the city?

a.   Patrick Henry
b.   George Wythe
c.   James Barbour
d.   Thomas Jefferson
e.   Thomas Nelson

* * * * *

4.   Who was the commander of the British force that captured Richmond?

a.   General Sir Charles Cornwallis
b.   General Henry Clinton
c.   General Benedict Arnold
d.   General John Burgoyne
e.   General Sir William Howe

* * * * *

5.   In the winter of 1918-19, _____ _____ swept the world, killing 500,000 people nation-wide, more than 50,000 in Virginia, including nearly 15,000 in Richmond.

* * * * *

6.   Which one of the following historical figures does not have a statue in Richmond?

a.   George Washington
b.   A.P. Hill

    c.   Arthur Ashe
    d.   Mathew Fontaine Maury
    e.   Winfield Scott

* * * * *

7.   True or false. Lee County is closer to three other state capitals than it is to Richmond.

* * * * *

8.   _____ of Richmond was the first woman to become a bank president in the U.S.

* * * * *

9.   The great evacuation fire of April 1865 that destroyed much of Richmond was started by which one of the following?

    a.   former slaves
    b.   federal troops bent on destruction
    c.   fleeing Confederate troops
    d.   carpetbaggers
    e.   none of the above

* * * * *

10.   Richmond became the capital of Virginia in 1780, the third community to serve in that role. _____ was the first capital, followed by _____.

* * * * *

11.   In 1948, which one of the following became the first African-American to be elected to the Richmond City Council since 1900?

    a.   Spotswood Robinson
    b.   Oliver W. Hill
    c.   Bill Robinson
    d.   John Mercer Langston
    e.   none of the above

* * * * *

12.   Virginia Commonwealth University claims 1838 as its founding date, when its medical college was established as a department of which one of the following schools?

    a.   Hampden-Sydney College
    b.   University of Virginia
    c.   Randolph-Macon College
    d.   College of William and Mary
    e.   none of the above

* * * * *

13.   If you drew a circle around Richmond with a 95-mile radius, how many U.S. presidents were born within it?

    a.   three
    b.   five
    c.   six
    d.   seven
    e.   eight
    f.   none of the above

* * * * *

14.   The Virginia Capitol has been home to the Virginia General Assembly since 1788. Only one other state capitol has been in use longer. Which of the following is it?

    a.   Annapolis, MD
    b.   Dover, DE
    c.   Boston, MA
    d.   Hartford, CT
    e.   none of the above

* * * * *

15.   Which future American president testified in the treason trial of Vice President Aaron Burr in Richmond in 1807?

    a.   James Monroe
    b.   Andrew Jackson
    c.   John Quincy Adams
    d.   James Madison
    e.   none of the above

* * * * *

To determine your grade, assign 6.5 points for each correct answer.
The grading scale is as follows:

90s -- You can teach the course.

80s -- You know enough to impress dinner guests.

70s -- You need a refresher.

60s -- Your brain is crowded with too much other information.

Below 60 -- Repeat the course.

Answers:

1.   b (Chimborazo)
2.   true (behind New Orleans and Charleston, SC)
3.   d
4.   c
5.   Spanish influenza
6.   e
7.   false (Charleston, WVA; Columbus, OH; Frankfort, KY.;
        Nashville TN; Columbia, SC, Atlanta, GA, Raleigh, NC
        and Indianapolis, IN)
8.   Maggie Walker
9.   c
10.   Jamestown, Williamsburg
11.   b
12.   a
13.   d (Washington, Jefferson, Madison, Monroe, W.H.
        Harrison, Tyler and Taylor. Wilson was born more than
        95 miles from Richmond, in Staunton.)
14.   a
15.   b

Richmond Times Dispatch, December 22, 2013

37

REVISIONISM ISN'T A DIRTY WORD
AND WHY WE NEED IT

A new exhibition at the Virginia Historical Society titled Lee and Grant reassesses the role that two men played in the preservation or disintegration of the United States. The show has received criticism from some quarters for comparing the lives of the ablest Union general and the South's greatest military commander, especially during the 200th anniversary of Robert E. Lee's birth. Several critics of the exhibition accuse its curators of "revisionism," a charge often leveled at any history that looks at the past in a new light.

I have just finished two excellent books published early this year that are revisionist: Elizabeth Pryor's *Reading the Man: Robert E. Lee Through His Private Letters* and Nelson Lankford's *Cry Havoc! The Crooked Road to Civil War, 1861.* Pryor takes a fresh look at Lee, having used a remarkable collection of Lee family papers acquired by the Historical Society a few years ago. Relying on a large body of recent scholarship, Lankford revisits the series of events, the key players, and the decisions they made leading up to the war.

These are familiar subjects to students of American history. During the years, hundreds of historians have examined and debated them. Pryor and Lankford continue that process, and each author's approach is unique. They remind us that history is not just a recitation of facts, dates, and events, a deadly boring method by which history often has been taught.

Good history is a constantly changing interpretation of the known facts, as long as those facts are not distorted to fit a particular point of view. Revisionism has become a dirty word to some people who inappropriately associate it with bad history.

On the contrary, the best historians, whether they are authors or museum curators, are revisionists. They do not just repeat what their predecessors have presented. They are always looking at familiar subjects from unique perspectives to come up with new ways of describing the past.Collections acquired by institutions such as the Historical Society often lead to fresh insights into events and people. Historians are not unlike detectives changing their analysis of a case based on recently uncovered evidence.

Journalists writing for different newspapers look at the same event and produce different stories. Interpreting history is no different. No two historians looking at a particular subject will bring it alive identically. Each perspective is unique and gives readers or museum visitors a novel perspective from that presented by previous historians.

These new books and the Historical Society's exhibition may differ from earlier interpretations of the Civil War, but that makes for more interesting and relevant history. If the definitive account had been written about Lee or Grant or the war, there would be no need for new books or exhibitions on these subjects. But authors, curators, and most importantly the reading public and museum visitors usually find that almost any topic, especially history, is more interesting and meaningful when seen in a contemporary light.

Richmond Times Dispatch, October 28, 2007

38

AT A CROSSROADS: TIME TO
TAP INTO RICHMOND'S HISTORY
(WITH BRENT GLASS)

I n the movie *Field of Dreams*, the character played by Kevin Costner hears a voice that inspires him to build a baseball field in an Iowa cornfield. People come in droves to watch old-timers play, a fantasy with a happy ending.

For history museums and sites, success in real life requires more than a Hollywood script. In Richmond, a proposed national slavery museum will need careful planning, broad public support and effective marketing. The idea is compelling, but if they build it, will people come—and will the museum be sustainable?

Last year, we co-authored a report on heritage tourism for Dr. Eugene Trani's Richmond's Future initiative. We evaluated the city's major historical assets and compared Richmond to several other state capitals.

We found that none surpasses Richmond's unique treasure trove of architectural landmarks and nationally significant histori-cal resources. It has abundant archival, library and artifact collec-tions that draw museum visitors, scholars and genealogists from across the country and around the world.

The proposed slavery museum, if built and sustained, could add to the richness of the historical attractions in the community. Richmond's historic resources have integrity and authenticity—two ingredients that are critical for an effective tourism initiative.

Draw a 75-mile radius around Richmond and you will not find another area in the country that is as steeped in the history of America. Stories of American Indians; the first permanent English settlement in America; the horrors of slavery; early representative government; the American Revolution; Founding Fathers and presidents; the Civil War; Reconstruction; the Industrial Revolution; World War II; the civil rights movement; and the Cold War are all within this remarkable circle.

Richmond's location at the interchange of two of the country's busiest interstate highways and within a day's drive of nearly one-third of the American population gives the city a strong competitive edge. It is not simple civic pride to proclaim Richmond as "the crossroads of American history."

The area's historic resources are being recognized by the travel industry, thanks in part to the efforts of Richmond Region Tourism to make history an important part of its marketing efforts.

The highly respected travel guide, *Frommer's*, recently named Richmond as one of its Top Destinations for 2014, commending the city for its historic attractions. The current Civil War sesquicentennial has helped increase visitation to the Richmond region.

Nevertheless, until relatively recently Richmond has not taken full advantage of its strengths and strategic opportunities, and it continues to trail other historic attractions. In Virginia Tourism Corporation's latest report, Richmond was not among the Top 25 Virginia Attractions Most Frequently Visited by Travelers, even though 16 of those were historic attractions and eight were Civil War sites.

Why? Part of problem is that despite the concerted efforts of Richmond Region Tourism to promote Richmond, the area trails other communities in funding for marketing. Richmond spends about $400,000 annually, while Virginia Beach; Atlanta; Nashville; Memphis; and Charleston each spend millions to promote tourism.

Because Richmond has a limited budget, targeting potential visitors is essential. Numerous studies reveal that interest in history grows with age. For various reasons, most people do not show an interest in the past until they become eligible for AARP membership.

Putting their own lives in perspective seems to become much more important. It is no surprise that the majority of subscribers to Ancestry.com, members of historical organizations, viewers of History on cable TV and PBS' *American Experience,* and readers of nonfiction history are people with graying hair.

With the baby-boom generation now reaching retirement age, Richmond has a resource -- history -- that should be tapped more effectively to attract this huge population. Boomers are traveling in large numbers, often with their children and grandchildren. The United States Tour Operators Association reported that half of its members report an increase in "grand travel" -- two- and three-generational trips instigated mostly by the grandparents.

We urge community leaders, tourism representatives and historic site directors and their boards to invest more in planning and promotion. A comprehensive heritage tourism plan would be crucial to a successful slavery museum. And let's spend some money to tell our story as "the crossroads of American history," an investment that can yield big dividends.

Brent D. Glass is director emeritus of the Smithsonian's National Museum of American History.

Richmond Times Dispatch, March 23, 2014

39

WHAT MAKES GREAT TEACHERS GREAT?
SEVEN CHARACTERISTICS

L ast year, our consulting firm assisted Hampden-Sydney College in developing a new strategic plan. Blessed with a dedicated faculty anchored in the liberal arts, Hampden-Sydney places special emphasis on teaching excellence, which can be defined many ways. One student's favorite professor may be another's nemesis. Yet there are certain teachers and college professors who are universally regarded as gifted in their craft.

A surprising number of people who have achieved success in life credit teachers with having opened their minds to new concepts and opportunities. As such "teachers are the most important people in our society," argues Pulitzer-Prize-winning author David McCullough.

What then constitutes a "great teacher?"

Our work at Hampden-Sydney made me particularly interested in that question. As a result, I interviewed a dozen current and former students from various schools, asking them to describe their favorite teachers or professors.

What made those teachers so good at their craft? The answers varied, but certain common traits emerged, seven in all.

My small sampling suggested that great teachers possess most of the following qualities:

1.   Love of Their Subject.

They love what they teach. That love is obvious and contagious, often rubbing off on students. Many of their students say, for example, "I really didn't like history until I took his class. Now I love it."

2.   Vibrant.

They are enthusiastic and energetic. Their classes are vibrant and lively, usually punctuated with regular give-and-take with students. Here the teaching process is a two-way street.

3.   Up-to-date.

Great teachers have complete command of their subject based on current scholarship, and they know how to present it in organized and understandable ways. There are no yellowed or dog- eared lecture notes in their classes. If they teach in technical fields, they stay abreast of constantly changing technology.

4.   Creative.

They are creative and help students look at things from different perspectives. They challenge assumptions and help students learn how to think analytically, critically, and to see things in a different light. Virginia's Standards of Learning testing requirements stifle creative teaching in public schools, according to many critics. A former high school principal, however, told me that the great teachers he knows have adapted to the SOLs and still do a superb job in the classroom.

5.   Demanding.

Great teachers usually are not easy teachers. They keep their students on their toes and do not pander to them. Yet they attempt to bring out the best in their students without badgering or humiliating them.

6.   Relevancy.

They have the ability to make their subject relevant so that students can see a connection to their own lives and the world around them.

7.   Trust.

Their credibility is unquestioned, and they are trusted by their students, who sense that the teacher is honest, forthright and fair.

Great teachers have the ability to change the lives of their students. A friend of mine was drifting aimlessly in college, not sure what she wanted to do. Then she took an elective course in accounting with no real motivation in mind. The professor presented the subject in such an interesting way that my friend was hooked and eventually became an executive at a major accounting firm.

Hampden-Sydney College President Christopher Howard recalls when he initially refused to read *Huckleberry Finn* in high school. As an African-American, he was convinced that it was a blatantly racist and degrading story. But Howard's English teacher persuaded him to give it a try. Initially reluctant, much to his surprise he found it to be a compelling story that took a scathing look at entrenched attitudes, particularly bigotry. Howard says that because of his teacher's insistence, he was given a lesson on how to judge for himself and apply critical thinking, both of which serve him well to this day.

David McCullough not only has the rare trait of being a hugely successful writer, but also is one of the most compelling public speakers of our time. He attributes his success at the podium to modeling himself after his art history professor at Yale, whose classes were always packed to overflowing.

In reviewing the traits associated with great teaching, it could be argued that those same characteristics can be applied to any number of jobs outside of the academic world. Whether in sales, law, personnel management, the ministry, the armed services and, yes, even accounting, having enthusiasm, love of one's profession, integrity, creativity and the ability to motivate others can serve almost anyone well.

People in professions outside the classroom, especially those in leadership positions, can also have a positive influence on those around them, and in that respect, they can be great teachers, too.

Richmond Times Dispatch, April 14, 2013

—∘∘—

40

WHAT UNIVERSITY PRESIDENTS NEED TO SUCCEED

I n recent years, we have witnessed numerous college and university leadership turnovers in Virginia. Some of those transitions have followed long and successful presidencies. Others, however, were brief and ended unhappily. Why? For one, the demands of the job are enormous, especially the never-ending fundraising pressure. The various constituencies who must be satisfied require skills that few people possess. Institutional cultures, personalities and leadership styles, financial conditions, the composition of the board, alumni demands and expectations, or the response to a crisis are often factors that determine whether a presidency ends with accolades or recriminations.

Last year I served as the consultant to the search committee in hiring Hampden-Sydney College's new president. After an extensive nationwide search, the board selected Dr. Christopher B. Howard, an exceptional candidate for the position. Early in the search, I called numerous college presidents seeking names of potential candidates. I also asked them to give me the traits that are essential to be successful at their jobs.

In all, I received many overlapping answers that I then consolidated into seven basic traits to help evaluate candidates. Ironically, fundraising ability did not make the list. That is intentional. Without most of the traits below college presidents cannot be as effective in that sphere. Those traits are:

1.   Integrity.

Probably the most important trait, all but two presidents I interviewed listed it or the word "credibility." University of Oklahoma president David Boren commented that without integrity, you cannot succeed as a leader. Some presidents have stretched it for short gains, only to see their support eventually erode. Once lost, integrity is hard to restore.

2.   Self-confidence without arrogance.

The personalities and leadership styles of college presidents vary widely, but the best ones understand that they cannot do it alone. Confident enough in themselves to build strong teams of leaders in key positions, they then allow the teams to do their jobs well without jealousy of their successes. They openly give credit where credit is due and accept blame for mistakes made.

3.   Listening and learning skills.

This trait is especially important in the early stages of a presidency. As one president said: "Consider yourself an anthropologist learning the tribal customs." Successful presidents ask lots of questions throughout their tenure, regularly measuring the pulse of the college and the environment in which it exists. They take a genuine interest in what makes it tick in all of its complexity. University of Richmond President Ed Ayers observed: "Universities are all about learning, and those who head them should never stop learning.

4.   Decision-making ability.

Almost every day, college presidents must make difficult decisions on a variety of issues. From crafting a budget to deciding on a thorny personnel problem, the final decision on many issues often lands on the president's desk. The most successful presidents are good at listening to other opinions, weighing the evidence at hand, and making decisions without extended delay. Anyone gripped with indecision will fail.

5.   Evident passion for the job.

Despite the difficulties associated with the position, successful presidents seem to thrive on their work, and are openly enthusiastic and passionate about the schools they head. Observers are wont to say, "She must love her job." The president's enthusiasm usually spreads to others who can help contribute to his or her success.

6.   The endurance of a triathlon athlete.

One college president compared the job to competing in a triathlon. Long hours, crowded schedules, often little time to catch your breath is the norm for college presidents. To do it well, the job must be held by people who can endure its physical and emotional demands without complaint or without bragging.

7.   Effective communication skills.

They have the ability to relate a compelling vision for their school in ways that inspire and motivate others to buy into it. Most are very good, but not necessarily great public speakers. Whether they are addressing a mass audience or speaking one-on-one, they command attention. As one college president observed: "Our most notable presidents - the Roosevelts, Reagan, Kennedy, Lincoln - were also great communicators."

Leaders of any kind, be they college presidents, corporate CEOs, or government officials could benefit from adopting these traits. Armed with them, the actions of such leaders can inspire others, especially students, to dream more, learn more, do more, and become more.

Richmond Times Dispatch, October 4, 2009

41

THOSE DISTINCTIVE VMI TYPES

P eople are occasionally surprised when I tell them that I graduated from the Virginia Military Institute. I don't know whether to take it as a compliment or an insult when they say I don't seem to be the "VMI type."

What is the VMI type? Is it represented by General George C. Marshall, VMI class of 1901, the only professional soldier to be awarded the Nobel Peace Prize? Does Jonathan Daniels, class of 1961, who was killed in 1965 saving the life of a fellow civil rights worker in Alabama, fit the profile? What about General John Jumper, class of '66, former chief of staff of the Air Force and now a Fortune 500 corporate chief executive? Does police officer Richard Donohue, class of 2002, who suffered a near-fatal wound during a shootout with the Boston Marathon bombing suspects last year?

Are Floyd and Bruce Gottwald -- classes of '43 and '54 respectively -- both highly successful captains of industry and philanthropists, "the type?" What about Ron Carter, class of 1978, a former NBA player who has been working in human and social services for the city of Chicago? Or Heidi Beemer, class of 2011, who is involved in helping establish a permanent colony on Mars? And is Fred Willard, class of 1955, a well-known movie and television comedy actor, the "VMI type?"

This year, VMI celebrates its 175th anniversary. Proclaiming that "the measure of a college lies in the quality and performance of its graduates and their contributions to society," the school's record of graduates who have distinguished themselves in a wide variety of endeavors can be matched by few colleges its size.

The unique VMI educational experience is often cited as the underlying reason for that record of achievement; yet it is a path toward a college degree that few people choose. The Institute does not hide from its reputation as a challenging and difficult school when it touts in a recruiting pitch that it is "no ordinary college, no ordinary life."

VMI distinctiveness becomes even more evident when you consider that Americans now have more than 1,500 colleges from which to choose. That number only counts four-year accredited institutions. The choices increase when the growing number of community colleges and for-profit universities are included.

For those who decide to go to VMI, the following four years often will be grueling. Their lives will be strictly regulated.

Their freshman or Rat year will be perhaps the most demanding time of their entire lives. One has to experience it to fully comprehend its difficulty. They will often think they are overwhelmed by the combination of academic requirements, military duties and the effort to be physically fit. They will be challenged to lead and to follow. Rarely will there be enough time in the day to get everything done. They will have to wear uniforms at all times, attend class, drill, suffer penalties for making mistakes, keep their rooms in order -- and do many things they would rather not. Professors will not cut them any slack in the classroom. Cadets must abide by one of the strictest honor codes in the country. Even the most motivated young men and women will sometimes question their reasons for being there.

Yet in return, most VMI graduates will have a sense of pride of accomplishment that will serve them well for the rest of their lives. They will develop bonds of friendship that transcend ordinary camaraderie. They will face future adversity with a degree of sangfroid that every cadet must have to get through VMI.

They will be almost compulsively punctual. Multitasking will come naturally to them. They will be honorable men and women who regard their integrity and credibility above anything else. They will tend to believe in service above self. Many of their fellow alums have paid the ultimate price of freedom in war -- far out of proportion to most other colleges. Let it be said, however, that while the majority of us who went to VMI think we are better for it, we are not better than graduates of other colleges. Our experience was simply different.

I am reminded of the words of my class valedictorian, Deaton Smith, at our graduation 45 years ago:

"Our VMI education has taught us that a life without a sense of responsibility is a life without meaning. It is in that respect that our education has been superior. We can only hope that the values of personal integrity and achievement will remain permanent features of our character."

Deaton died recently after a long battle with cancer, following a distinguished career as an emergency room physician. He was the "VMI type" too.

Happy 175th, VMI.

* For reader reaction to this essay, see page 270.

Richmond Times Dispatch, April 27, 2014

42

A Forgotten Virginia Thanksgiving Tradition: The VMI vs VPI Football Game

To this day, I have trouble rooting for Virginia Tech in football. I admit that their Hokies are to be admired for many reasons. Under the leadership of legendary coach Frank Beamer, Tech has developed into one of the country's elite football programs.

But I cannot forget that this perennial football power was once the most intense rival of my *alma mater*, the Virginia Military Institute. Ask people what is the premier sports rivalry in Virginia today, and most will say it is between Tech and the University of Virginia.

Courtesy of the VMI archives

For those of us who have reached the half-century mark in life, however, the great rivalry once was between Tech and VMI. From 1913 to 1973, the schools met annually in Roanoke in an event that was a central component of Thanksgiving for many Virginia families. A poster from the 1930's proclaimed the gridiron face-off as the "Biggest Day of the Year in Virginia." Known then as "The Military Classic of the South," it made the cover of *Sports Illustrated* in 1959.

Today Virginia Tech and VMI are vastly different schools, but they were remarkably alike for nearly six decades. VMI was founded in 1839 in Lexington, and offered an education to young men modeled after the United States Military Academy at West Point. Never a large school, its graduates have served with distinction in both the military and civilian world.

Seventy-five miles southwest in Blacksburg, the Virginia Agricultural and Mechanical College (later changed to the Virginia Polytechnic Institute, and now simply Virginia Tech) was founded as a military school in 1871. The all male student body was organized into a corps of cadets who lived in a strict military environment.

Although the two schools were already rivals of sorts in the late nineteenth century because of their common military nature, the introduction of American football as an official team sport at VMI and VPI in the 1890's intensified the competition. In 1894, they faced off for the first time in Staunton, with VMI winning 10 to 6. Two years later, they met on Thanksgiving Day in Roanoke, with the boys from Blacksburg slamming VMI 24 to 0. Beginning in 1913, the game became an annual Thanksgiving ritual in Roanoke.

Nothing can match the pageantry of the Army-Navy Game, but the VMI-VPI gridiron clash came close. Excitement mounted leading up to the game, especially within the two corps. They often played pranks on each other, dropping inflammatory leaflets from low flying planes on their rival's campus, leaving insulting messages on their opponent's campus landmarks, or capturing the other school's mascot.

On game day, the respective corps rose early, ate breakfast, boarded trains (buses in later years) for the hour-long trek to Roanoke. When they arrived, cadets from both schools mingled briefly on the streets, warily eyeing each other while critiquing the appearance of the opposite corps. Even the most laid back VPI or VMI cadet made sure his shoes were shined to a high gloss, as was any brass on his uniform.

Soon bugles blew and the two corps formed up to march into Victory Stadium. Proud parents, siblings, girlfriends, alumni, politicians, and people with no connection to either school crowded the sidewalks to watch the cadets march behind their respective bands as they blared out lively renditions of "Tech Triumph" and "VMI Spirit."

The respective cadet corps alternated years marching in first. Dressed in their long overcoats (cadet gray for VMI, army blue for VPI) with scarlet capes pulled back, both corps represented the pride of Virginia. No other state had anything like this spectacle.

Once in opposite stands, cadets stood the whole game and yelled themselves hoarse cheering their respective teams to victory. In its heyday, the stadium was filled with more than 20,000 spectators. In the first three decades of the rivalry, the winning records were fairly even, but gradually Tech pulled ahead and eventually ruled the series. By the time the annual game ended in 1973, the record was 49-25-5 in Tech's favor.

The dominance of the Hokies reflected a significant transformation of the school's mission to become a large research university. The size and make-up of its student body underwent significant changes. Women began attending VPI in the 1920's but were not allowed to join the corps. Eventually, membership in the corps became optional for all students. Enrollment soared, reaching 10,000 by the mid-1960's, and doubling again in the next decade.

Tech's student body became increasingly civilian. With a pervasive anti-military climate in America after the Vietnam War, its corps, once larger than VMI's, dropped below a thousand cadets. Tech also moved its competition in football up several levels by taking on teams of other large universities. Few of its athletes were members of the corps. The "Military Classic of the South" became an anachronism.

VMI, on the other hand, kept its student population to only 1,200 cadets. Unlike Tech, its athletes continued to live in a strict military environment, making recruiting an increasing challenge.

The two teams clashed for the last time on the gridiron in Norfolk in 1984, with Tech steamrolling VMI 54 to 7, a score indicative of just how different the once comparable rivals had become.

During my four years at VMI, Tech won three of four games by a combined score of 189 to 45. We beat the Hokies 12 to 10 in a stunning upset my junior year, denying them a bowl bid. Tech extracted revenge on us the next year 55 to 6. That was nearly 50 years ago, and I still haven't gotten over it.

Richmond Times Dispatch, November 23, 2014

43

RESURRECTIONS AND SHAKEDOWNS:
A NEVER FORGOTTEN VMI EXPERIENCE

When VMI alumni gather, we inevitably turn the conversation to our cadet days, especially our experiences as Rats (freshmen). We laugh at long-ago incidents that were awful at the time, but seem hilarious now.

I do not know how or when the term "Resurrection" originated at VMI, but these two to three day ordeals were a mainstay of the Rat experience half a century ago. Administered by first classmen (seniors) when it was thought the Rats were becoming too uppity, resurrections were supposed to whip the fourth classmen (another name for freshmen) back into their humble place in the corps. These crackdowns tested the mental and physical endurance of anyone who experienced them. The fact that we were taking a full load of college classes made no difference, and only added to the stress. During Resurrections, from the moment we woke in the morning until taps, we suffered through sweat parties, laps around the parade ground toting our rifles until we nearly collapsed, and meals with upper classmen yelling at us with every bite we took. Then there were shakedowns, ordeals that often served as the opening event of a Resurrection.

I remember one shakedown in particular. It came soon after the start of second semester, late January or early February of 1966, a time for which I have no fond memories. It was bitterly cold. A deep, hardened blanket of snow covered the parade ground. The stark interior of barracks resembled a grim, gray grotto. Christmas furlough had faded away into distant memory—a temporary reverie that had gone by all too quickly. We had just wrapped up first semester exams, the results for which were less than stellar for me. My squad leader and his sidekick and assistant squad leader continued to prove their mettle as two of the worst persecutors of Rats in the corps. I was on academic probation, writing off for catalogs to transfer to a college that had good looking women rather than sadistic upper classmen.

The last notes of taps had long sounded, lights were out, and barracks had settled into its nightly silent mode. In Room 405, my two roommates and I had fallen into a deep sleep, just about our only escape from the grind of the Ratline. The only sounds were the subtle hiss of the radiator and the gentle snores emanating from the room's three occupants. I had probably gone to sleep mulling over the next day's humiliation in front of the chalk board trying to explain a chemistry problem handed to me by the professor.

Suddenly, we were jolted awake to a living nightmare as we heard faint but menacing noises of doors being kicked in, followed by angry shouted commands that worked their way down the stoop like an approaching torpedo amidships. Then, all of a sudden, "Boom!" our door flew open, blinding fluorescent light flooded the room, and two first classmen wearing gray blouses stormed in and shouted: "Get up, Rats, and start double timing!" They immediately ordered us to put our hay racks up, not an easy task while double timing.

In the meantime, other menacing upper classmen dashed in and out of our room, each taking his turn trashing it. They dumped our laundry bag contents on the floor, pulled our neatly folded shirts, underwear, and socks from our presses and flung them every which way. They threw the contents of our miscellaneous boxes all over the floor. That's when it got interesting.

Earlier that day, one of my roommates had received a delicious pineapple upside down cake from his mother. Somehow we had eaten only about a fourth of it. It didn't take long for that delicacy to land on the floor. I remember as if it were today the feeling of my constantly pumping bare feet smashing into that cake, and the cold, slick pieces of pineapple and moist cake oozing between my toes. Amidst the double timing, pushups, and other tortures being inflicted on us, Rich and Larry also "sampled" some of the cake with their bare feet.

After what seemed like an hour—it was probably no more than 15 minutes—the upper classmen turned our lights out, ordered us back to bed, and then left us with the sweet dreams wish of "Get this room in SMI (Sunday Morning Inspection) condition by first call in the morning!" In other words, immaculate.

I'm not sure who was room orderly, but all three of us, soaking with sweat, tried to make order out of the chaos in the dark. We did the best we could with the room, and then finally collapsed back into our hays totally exhausted.

No doubt I embarrassed myself on that chemistry board problem the next morning. How I was able to stay in school is a wonder, but I, along with nearly half of my class, ended up on academic probation by the end of the semester. It is little wonder that summer school at VMI thrived in those days. I did my part to add to the revenue stream of VMI's summer school budget for two years in a row.

Resurrections and those shakedowns were no fun, and when we broke out of the Ratline, I'm sure we thought we would never experience them again. Little did we realize then that if you live long enough, resurrections and the shakedowns don't end; they come in different forms instead—experiencing combat, going through a divorce, being fired from a job, losing a loved one to death, or contracting a dreaded disease.

I doubt there is a VMI alumnus who hasn't experienced one or more of those later-day resurrections. But like the ones of our time at VMI, we survived them, got on with it, and tried to put our lives in SMI order as soon as possible. It's one of those aspects of our unique college experience that anyone outside of our circle is challenged to comprehend. In a perverse way, it has served us well. I must confess, however, that to this day I cannot eat pineapple upside down cake.

First time published. This essay was written for my Brother Rats (classmates) from the Class of 1969.

44

MAJOR LEAGUE MUSEUMS:
EVEN WITHOUT THE BRAVES,
THE BOULEVARD IS BLESSED

W hen I consult with organizations involved in long-range planning, I always pose a question: "If, for any reason, your organization ceased operating or left this community, would people care and would it make any difference in their lives?" If the answer is "probably not," that organization must work harder to make itself relevant.

Unfortunately, Richmond is about to lose an important organization. Following extended public debate over construction of a new baseball stadium at taxpayer expense, the news of next year's departure of the Richmond Braves has been a blow to the collective ego of the people of our region. Unless a replacement team can be recruited, our city faces the loss of nearly 350,000 fans annually, along with millions of dollars in revenue that the Braves have generated. Relevant to the question I posited above, lots of people do care and the loss of the Braves will make a difference. Plenty of finger-pointing is going on among embarrassed public officials to assess blame.

Fortunately, Richmond will remain one of America's most livable cities even without the Braves. In recent years, numerous surveys have ranked us high in "livability" among American cities because of a number of factors - climate, affordable housing, a diverse economy, and fine cultural amenities, among others. Ironically, the presence of professional sports has never been listed.

I'm afraid we take for granted many of the factors that make our community great. Let me cite one in particular - museums. Even though we will be losing minor league baseball, we are still blessed with major league museums. Indeed, compared to most American cities its size, our metropolitan area has an unusually large number of museums and historical institutions. There are 30 in all, some of which are regarded by their peers as among the best in the country. On the Boulevard alone—a cultural corridor often compared to the Smithsonian-lined Mall in Washington—the collection of first-class museums and parks that educate the public about history, art, science, and the natural world is rarely found elsewhere.

Dozens of other area museums and historic sites help interpret many important aspects of American history. The vast collection of historic materials, artifacts, and works of art that our museums house and display contain some of America's great treasures. Think how fortunate students and teachers in area schools and beyond are to have these great museums and their collections open and available to enhance learning outside the classroom.

While the cultural, educational, and stewardship roles of area museums play a crucial part in the quality of life in Richmond, their economic impact on the community is no less significant. In 2007, our museums attracted some 2.7 million visitors, nearly eight times the number of fans who attend Braves games during a season. And over the past decade alone, new museum construction and other capital improvements have totaled more than a quarter-billion dollars, little of which has come from local government funding.

Despite the vital role they play in the life of the community, our museums have never received significant financial support from local government when compared to many other American cities. Although money for marketing area museum attractions has increased in recent years, it trails that of comparable locales. How many of us have met people who say they've traveled through Richmond on their way to attractions and historic sites elsewhere? Or that they didn't realize there was anything worth seeing in Richmond?

If more local support was invested in our area museums, the return would be much greater than we receive now. With the

150th anniversary of the Civil War less than three years away, Richmond could reap significant dividends during the following four years if we can only get the word out better than we do now.

Back to my opening question. What if our area museums ceased operation or left Richmond like the Braves? Would people care and would it make any difference in their lives? For the hundreds of thousands of school kids and their teachers; for the many area hotel and restaurant owners and their workers; for the countless number of people considering a move to Richmond who are studying its quality of life; and for everyone who enjoys world-class exhibitions, stimulating lectures, innovative programs for children, and the opportunity to commune with nature in a beautiful setting, the answer would be a resounding "Yes!"

Richmond Times Dispatch, March 31, 2008

45

THE DANGERS OF DENYING HARD HISTORY—MODERN GERMANY COMES TO GRIPS WITH THE HOLOCOST

Denial comes in many forms. Alcoholics often deny their problem. People sometimes refuse to admit certain unpleasant aspects of their past. Perhaps it is a defensive mechanism for us to disconnect ourselves from those things that put us in an unfavorable light, even though we are not responsible for the events and actions of our forebears.

I was reminded of this during a recent river cruise from Amsterdam to Budapest. From visiting the Anne Frank house in Amsterdam to seeing statuary in Cologne pockmarked with shrapnel from bombing raids, it was still easy to find the evidence of World War II all along our route.

As we headed up the Main River through the bucolic German countryside, I thought of the American GIs, including my late father-in-law, who in April 1945 began to discover a form of evil that even those combat-hardened veterans could not imagine.

In a camp outside of Dachau, near Munich, they saw people barely covered in filthy rags, so emaciated that they seemed little more than walking skeletons. Stacks of dead Jews lay everywhere, left scattered by their German guards who had hastily escaped before the arrival of the American army. Cremation ovens containing human remains only added to the horror of what the Americans witnessed.

Many of those GIs wondered how the German people could allow such evil to exist within their midst. How could they blindly fall under the spell of Adolf Hitler, who plunged them into a war that ultimately led to the virtual destruction of their nation? This was, after all, a nation that produced some of the world's greatest musicians, philosophers, scientists and writers.

In visits to Germany years ago, I often observed denial of what had happened during the war. I remember asking a guide why her town showed little indication of wartime bombing. I still doubt her answer that it had been anti-Nazi.

Another German told me that his history teachers routinely ended their lessons at World War I, choosing not to go further into the darker side of their nation's past. Other Germans confirmed that their early schooling in history failed to come to grips with the nation's World War II experience. As one man my age said, "Perhaps it was too painful or embarrassing for our teachers to discuss."

That refusal to face the unpleasant aspects of the past seems to have diminished now. The Bamberg city hall, for example, houses a forthright exhibition describing the rise of the Nazis in the community, the persecution of local Jews and the devastation the community suffered from bombing raids during the war. A large museum in Nuremberg devoted to the disturbing story of Nazi Germany was filled with visitors, including schoolchildren.

I was told that German students must now visit at least one Holocaust-related site, and *The Diary of Anne Frank* is required reading for middle-schoolers. Perhaps the greatest irony is the change in certain street names near the arena where Hitler held those vast Nazi Party rallies in the 1930s. The streets are now named to honor former Israeli prime ministers.

All of this made me think about my native South and its most wrenching experience. The story of Nazi Germany is not the same as that of the Confederacy and our Civil War. The Confederacy ordered no mass genocide of a certain part of its population, nor did it have any ambition to rule the world. The Southern people did not fall under the spell of a demagogue.

There are similarities, however. Like post-World War II Germany, the South was laid waste in 1865. A sizable portion of its male population was dead. A persecuted segment of the population was freed. Civilians were not immune to the devastation of war.

And like Germans, who for decades denied what their country had done, many white Southerners refused to accept the reality that slavery was the root cause of the Civil War and that the right side eventually won.

Today, cries that "the South shall rise again" ring more hollow than they once did. Streets formerly lined only with Confederate memorials now recognize heroes who descended from slaves. The current Civil War sesquicentennial commemoration has successfully embraced the full story of probably the most tragic period in our nation's history, a far cry from the almost celebratory atmosphere of the war's centennial 50 years ago.

I do not agree fully with the sentiments of the eighteenth-century British historian Edward Gibbon, who opined that essentially "history is the register of the crimes, follies and misfortunes of mankind." On the other hand, to ignore the unpleasant realities of the past is the ultimate form of denial.

Richmond Times Dispatch, May 20, 2012

Part V

The Way Things Were

Arguably the world changed more in the twentieth century than any previous century. This was true of the United States and especially Virginia. Arnold Toynbee once observed that the chief characteristic of Virginia was its resistance to change. But even it was able to resist change only so much.

At the beginning of the century, nearly 80 percent of the American people lived in rural areas and were involved in farming or farm-related work. By the year 2000, only about ten percent of the American population lived in rural areas, and only about five percent were involved in agriculture. Despite that dramatic drop in farm workers, the nation more than doubled its agricultural output from 1900 to 2000.

Most Americans had never traveled farther than a hundred miles from home, yet by 1969, two of their own left footprints on the moon. With great advances in medicine, the average lifespan of an American nearly doubled in the twentieth century. The way of communicating with their fellow human beings changed from the hand written word to the spoken word and then back to the written word sent electronically.

I could go on about how things changed in the twentieth century and how the pace of change continues unabated in the twenty-first. Suffice it to say it will not slow down. The following essays touch the surface of only some of the things that were important agents of change

46

WHEN RADIO WAS THE LATEST THING

Our handheld communication devices can retrieve news from around the globe almost as it happens. But only within the past century and a half have we been able to receive far-flung information so rapidly. Radio played a key early role in that development, and it greatly influenced the world as we know it today.

We rarely think about the ubiquitous radio now, but for people living a century ago it was a marvel. Pioneered by Italian Guglielmo Marconi in the 1890s, early radio messages were basically wireless transmissions sent out in Morse code.

The world's first voice transmissions, however, were perfected and broadcast in America in the early 1900s by the U.S. Weather Bureau. Lack of adequate funding and ongoing technical problems plagued the endeavor, but broadcasts continued sporadically for years.

The Navy opened a small station in Virginia in 1913 that delivered weather updates and general information over the airwaves to anyone who could receive it, many at great distances. A massive ice storm destroyed the station, however, forcing it to close permanently in 1920.

Within a few years, radio broadcasting in America changed significantly. Government sponsorship and control of the medium that had been instituted during World War I was withdrawn. Unlike other nations, America transferred the operation of its radio system to private enterprise. With limited government control, large corporations such as Westinghouse, RCA and several insurance companies established stations that eventually dominated the airwaves.

In an event that garnered national publicity, America's first commercial radio station, KDKA in Pittsburgh, broadcast the results of Warren Harding's election as president in 1920. It also aired recorded and live music to a growing audience. KDKA's success started a race to build broadcasting stations -- and people rushed to buy radios.

Radio became a national craze. In 1922 alone, the number of licensed stations jumped from four to 576. Seven stations were established in Virginia, including Richmond's first, WQAT, followed by WRVA in 1925, marking Virginia's most ambitious entry into the world of radio. Owned by Larus & Brothers, a tobacco company, WRVA's mighty 1,000-watt signal (later expanded to 50,000 watts) reached great distances. Powerful stations like WRVA -- WSM in Nashville, WLS in Chicago, WBZ in Boston, WWL in New Orleans, and KMOX in St. Louis -- beamed their signals to millions of listeners throughout the nation.

At first, the only listening devices were homemade crystal sets employing earphones. Soon, superior tube sets replaced crystal units, and transmitters grew more powerful. People hosted radio parties. Rural folk gathered in country stores to listen to far-off voices and popular melodies.

By 1930, a third of American homes had radios, a number that soared to 86 percent in the next decade despite the Great Depression. The influence of radio was immense. President Franklin Roosevelt used it effectively in his "fireside chats" to promote his policies. In Europe, Adolph Hitler and Benito Mussolini rose to power in part because they were able to reach the masses over the airwaves.

Popular culture was greatly affected by radio's ability to allow geographically dispersed Americans to share in common experiences, especially with the establishment of large networks such as NBC and CBS. Radio commercials influenced buying habits. Radio could cause mass panic, as it did the night of Orson Welles' broadcast of *The War of the Worlds*, convincing listeners that a fictional invasion by Martians in New Jersey was real.

Today's public obsession with celebrities and sports stars can be traced in part to early radio. Popular musicians such as

Benny Goodman and Glenn Miller achieved unprecedented star status. Country music flourished over the airwaves with the broadcast of the Grand Ole Opry on WSM in Nashville and WRVA's Old Dominion Barn Dance. The reputations of the great sports heroes of the time -- Babe Ruth, Red Grange and Bobby Jones -- were enhanced by the medium. It helped make Charles Lindbergh a household name overnight.

Radio also affected the way people disseminated and obtained information. After the United States entered World War II, Americans tuned into their radios to learn about the latest breaking news from far-flung battlefields.

After the war, however, radio began to lose some of influence when another powerful medium, television, emerged. Like the rapid increase in radio listeners in the 1930s, television sales boomed two decades later. Advertising dollars, the lifeblood of newspapers and radio, began to shift to the new visual medium. The "Golden Age of Radio" soon ended.

Over the millennia, the world gradually became smaller as transportation routes, both on land and sea, were developed. These, in turn, gradually increased the dissemination of information. The advent of radio a century ago, however, made transportation routes irrelevant when it came to circulating information and shaping public opinion. Once radio became universally established, the world has never been the same.

Richmond Times Dispatch, April 6, 2014

47

EVOLVING HISTORY: AMERICAN NEWSPAPERS

W hether you are reading this column from a newspaper or a computer screen, you are participating in an activity that has been a hallmark of the American republic even before its founding.

American colonists started reading their own newspapers in 1703, when printed news got its start in Boston. By the 1730s, Virginia's earliest newspaper, *The Gazette*, began publication in Williamsburg. On the eve of the Revolution, some two dozen newspapers were active throughout the colonies. Many of these newspapers moved American opinion toward independence from Great Britain.

By war's end, the number of newspapers had increased to 43 -- and to 350 two decades later.

What explains the growth in the print medium? Lack of government control was crucial. With the first article of the Bill of Rights guaranteeing freedom of the press, newspapers could express divergent views on a variety of issues. As a result, they assumed a central role in national affairs and in shaping public attitudes.

Publishers found an eager readership that mirrored the emergence of political factions in the young republic. Early journalists pulled few punches, often making statements that would be regarded as libelous today. Political factions owned many newspapers outright and were blatantly partisan in what they printed, a practice that continued well into the nineteenth century.

Revenue from advertisements proved lucrative, which in turn led to an increase in newspapers as profit-making businesses.

Starting with simple notices from lawyers, merchants, shipping companies and public officials, advertisements quickly became the leading revenue source for newspapers. Escaped slave ads provided significant funding for the print media until the end of that institution during the Civil War.

Increasing literacy and the advent of the "penny presses" led to an even greater expansion of papers. By the mid-nineteenth century, the United States had one of the most literate citizenries in the world, although limited mainly to its white population.

Improvements in the printing process, along with the invention of inexpensive wood-pulp-based paper, revolutionized the newspaper industry. Large, powerful steam-driven presses, able to pour out hundreds, even thousands of issues, began to replace slower manual versions.

Newspapers now could be sold for as little as one cent. These penny-press journals became available to anyone who could read, almost regardless of economic status. Cheap and filled with interesting -- often salacious -- stories, they reached a vast readership.

By 1850, nearly 2,500 papers were being published nationwide. It was not unusual for cities to have multiple journals, both morning and evening versions. At the beginning of the Civil War, for example, Richmond boasted four daily papers, a number that increased to six by 1864. An unprecedented demand for timely, accurate news from the front contributed to this growth. For the first time, "specials" -- now called reporters -- prepared detailed accounts of campaigns and battles, a practice that transformed American journalism. Newspapers also began to carry engraved images that allowed readers to visualize people and events for the first time. The print medium grew unabated after the war, and by the 1880s newspapers numbered 11,000 nationwide. Well into the twentieth century newspapers continued to thrive; but with the advent of radio and television, circulation began to decline.

People no longer depended on the print media as their only source of current events, especially breaking news, which was conveyed more quickly by the broadcast media. By the 1970s, television became the primary source of news for Americans.

Newspapers began to disappear, especially afternoon journals like *The Richmond News Leader*. People commuting from work could listen to the latest news on their car radios and turn on their TV once home, rather than open a paper. Television began to capture bigger audiences, along with the advertising dollars newspapers had relied on.

While television news attracted more and more Americans, the Internet was an even greater threat to print journalism. With its advent, almost unlimited amounts of up-to-date information was available free of charge. Not wanting to become an anachronism, newspapers started websites that, for all intents and purposes, gave away their most important commodity -- news -- for free. Some observers argue that this has been a fatal mistake. Once-loyal newspaper readers began to access free online news.

The slow economy of recent years has only added to the problem. Print ads, long the revenue lifeblood of American newspapers, have declined precipitously, and shifted to the broadcast media and the Internet.

Are newspapers dying? Not in other parts of the world. Papers in Europe have fared better because they are less reliant on advertising revenue. Growing demand in emerging markets such as India, Indonesia and Brazil has led to a 35 percent increase in circulation over the past decade, thanks in part to less government oversight, increased literacy and improved financial circumstances for their citizens.

Many experts argue that a new business model is needed in the United States. Others contend that the print media are not dying but simply evolving into a new form. Whether it is delivered on paper or electronically, uncensored, up-to-date and informative news will continue to be the bedrock of the American democratic experience.

Richmond Times Dispatch, October 7, 2012

48

WEATHER: ONCE A MATTER
OF LIFE AND DEATH

For the most part, we take winter weather for granted. It has become so predictable that well-trained meteorologists using sophisticated computer and satellite technology can accurately forecast conditions for tomorrow or the next ten days.

We are warned of impending snow, floods or dangerously low temperatures. We live in homes and travel in vehicles that are climate-controlled. Most of us work indoors, cocooning ourselves from both the extremes of winter and summer.

Ironically, winters of old are often portrayed romantically in Currier & Ives prints of New England village snow scenes or in the gleeful lyrics of *Jingle Bells*. In reality, however, winter was a season of discontent until relatively recently.

The way we experience it now cannot compare to what our ancestors endured. Today, weather is more of a temporary inconvenience. For most of history, however, winter was often a life-or-death matter. A nineteenth century commentator contended that "anyone who passes a winter's day has escaped an enemy."

The infamous blizzard of March 1888 is a perfect example. A powerful Arctic blast roared across the Great Plans, swept into the Midwest and eventually dumped heavy snow on the East Coast. Nearly 2,000 people died across the country, hundreds in New York City, which had 20 inches of snow in one night. More than 30,000 cattle froze to death on the Plains. Commerce was shut down for weeks.

Were winters of the past harsher? The first carefully chronicled meteorological records from the late eighteenth century suggest that they were.

George Washington, the consummate farmer, kept a detailed weather diary from 1767 to 1799, always mindful of the effect of the elements on his crops. Thomas Jefferson was fascinated with weather and recorded meticulous temperature and barometric readings, as did James Madison. Between their diaries and brief newspaper accounts, we have a good picture of Virginia weather patterns from the late eighteenth century on.

Their entries reveal some astonishing weather phenomena. In January 1772, Washington recorded three feet of snow at Mount Vernon and that "the snow was up to the breast of a tall horse everywhere."

At the same time, Jefferson was returning to Monticello with his new bride, when bad weather set in. They were forced to abandon their carriage and barely made it home. Madison noted an 18-inch accumulation of snow in Norfolk.

What made winters so difficult? First was their unpredictability. Unlike today, when accurate forecasts can extend weeks ahead, this was not the case until the twentieth century. The consequences were profound. With no knowledge of impending bad weather, beginning in November until the following spring, people curtailed travel, and economic activities slowed down.

Presidential inaugurations were delayed until March in consideration of the weather and travel time to the capital. During war, maneuvers were restricted. Most armies went into winter quarters because nature could disrupt the most carefully laid plans.

Everyday life was especially difficult. With no insulation, homes were frigid and drafty. During cold snaps, one could see his breath while indoors. Thick sheets of ice formed on the inside of window panes. Children often slept several to a bed just for warmth.

People relied mostly on fireplaces, one of the most inefficient heating methods, to combat the freezing temperatures. Free-standing stoves and home furnaces gradually gained usage in the nineteenth century, limited at first to the wealthy.

Travel could be difficult, unbearably cold, and dangerous. Roads and streets were not cleared, making navigation extremely difficult. Horses required special care. Wagons became all but use-less. People living in rural areas could be snowbound for weeks on end.

Winter was also a time of death, not from freezing but from illness. Pneumonia was the great killer of young and old alike. During America's early wars, soldiers died by the thousands in winter camps rather than on the battlefield.

Fortunately, much has changed for the better. Homes are built and equipped to provide havens from the extremes of summer and winter alike. Roads are cleared quickly after snowfalls so that we can take our comfortable vehicles to almost any place we want. Forecasting has been so fine-tuned that weather surprises are increasingly rare.

Something else has occurred-- fewer long, severe winters. Average winter temperatures have risen steadily for a century, reinforcing arguments that global warming is real.

In recent years, mild winters make the period between November and March less ominous than it once was. While our forebears dreaded winter, the time may come when snowstorms, frigid temperatures and the disruptions they cause may become even less frequent. Is that a good thing? Something tells me no.

Richmond Times Dispatch, April 28, 2013

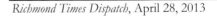

49
IS THE ART OF LETTER WRITING DYING?

Recently my wife and I gave our attic a long overdue downsizing. We hauled several truckloads of stuff to Goodwill and the dump. It was a physically exhausting but rewarding experience that took us on a nostalgic journey into our past. As we opened box after box, I was reminded that attics are our personal archives and museums. As we worked I was excited to find two boxes of letters mostly between us when I was a VMI cadet and she was a student at Mary Baldwin College.

Soon after finishing in the attic, I started reading the letters spanning from October 1966 to the spring of 1969. They chronicle a different world from that of young people today. Text messaging, e-mails, Facebook, Twitter, Skype, and cell phones were far into the future. Long-distance phone calls were expensive then and rarely made. So, we handwrote lots and lots of letters to each other-hundreds. As a historian, I have read countless old letters, giving me insight into the lives of other people and their times. Now I was peering into my own long ago life.

Cammy Martin (Bryan) and the author, Spring of 1967.

Our letters tell the story of two young people falling in love, worrying about grades and exams, scheduling dates, bragging about their tans, suffering through stifling summer heat without air conditioning, and making plans for the future. Like almost every cadet before and after me, I griped frequently about VMI. After being slapped with demerits, penalty tours, and confinement for rust on my rifle, I exclaimed: "It's times like this that I hate this place!"

Most of the letters discussed our daily routines and had their share of mushy prose, but events of a tumultuous time appeared frequently in our words. Knowing I would enter the Army after VMI, the war in Vietnam hung ominously over our future. We commented on assassinations and race riots. We described heated political debates with our roommates.

The last letters in the collection reflected the anticipation and excitement we felt as our wedding approached after my VMI graduation. Once we married, however, our correspondence ended. The number of letters to my family and friends also began to drop. Why?

It is no coincidence that my diminished correspondence followed a national trend. Recently the U.S. Postal Service announced that the amount of first-class mail delivery has dropped 22 percent since 1996. As is often the case, new, easier, and cheaper ways of communicating such as the Internet and cellular phones accelerated a growing trend away from letterwriting.

The decline actually started with the introduction of microwave relays and fiber-optic connections in the 1970s, helping make long-distance phone calling more efficient and less expensive. The court-ordered break-up of AT&T ("Ma Bell") in 1982 led to increased competition among long-distance providers, resulting in significant reductions in rates. With low-cost long-distance calling now available, it became easier to "reach out and touch someone" by phone as a then-popular AT&T commercial proclaimed. I, like most Americans, started calling more and writing less. Cell phones have accelerated that process. With rare exception, there is no record of our phone conversations.

Ironically, with the advent of e-mail and other electronic formats, we can connect with people almost anywhere in writing.

But most e-mails are quickly composed, ephemeral messages, lacking the thought and feeling that go into a written letter. Retention of electronic communication is another issue. We eventually delete most of our messages to free up space on our computers. Unless we make hard copies, most of them are gone forever.

Historians are concerned that the demise of traditional writing will affect the way the past is researched and interpreted in the future. Written documents, the most important means of communication for ages, have provided scholars with a unique view of history that other evidence simply cannot yield. How will future historians reconstruct our times from e-mail which is often fleeting and short-lived? The situation is serious enough that projects such as George Mason University's Center for History and New Media are under way to preserve and present electronic documentation.

I realize that there are upsides and downsides to technological advances, but nothing substitutes for the richness of information that a good collection of letters contains, like those treasures I rediscovered in our attic. I'm afraid, however, that letter writing is a dying art and something is being lost in the process.

Richmond Times Dispatch, January 10, 2010

50

CROSSING THE COUNTRY IN STYLE
IN 1962, A REMEMBRANCE

In 2012, my son and I drove from Washington state to his home in North Carolina. Our trip reminded me of my first trip to the West when I joined my uncle's family on a grand excursion to the Seattle World's Fair in 1962.

We left their home in Mississippi and drove to Southern California, then on up to Seattle. After two days at the fair, we headed back across the country, arriving home after traveling 6,200 miles in three weeks and having visited various sites in fifteen states and one Canadian province.

Some key differences marked my two trips. My son and I dressed casually in shorts and golf shirts. Photos of my 1962 trip show that we three teenagers frequently dressed casually for the time. My uncle, however, usually wore dress slacks and shirt, while my aunt always wore a dress.

A nondescript Honda Civic that consumed about 35 mpg served as our means of transport in 2012. Fifty years earlier, we cruised along in my uncle's gargantuan 1959 Cadillac, which sported huge sharp tailfins, bullet-shaped taillights and a jeweled rear grill. That pale yellow behemoth gulped a gallon of gas every ten miles.

My uncle did all the driving, which was a challenge in 1962. Interstate highways were few then, so most of our journey was on standard four- and two-lane highways. Poor roads sometime slowed us.

When we headed up steep mountains on two-lane roads, we inevitably slowed to turtlelike speed behind big trucks spewing

The Bryan Family in their '59 Cadillac somewhere in Montana on or around June 14, 1962. The author, in the cowboy hat, and his cousins Bill Bryan and Becky Bryan (now Becky Allen) stopped for a break as they headed back east after a visit to the Seattle World's Fair.

diesel fumes in their path. My uncle anxiously waited for a short straight stretch of road to gun it past the truck before an oncoming vehicle appeared. It is little wonder that head-on collisions were more common in those days.

Where to dine or spend the night was a challenge. There were few restaurant chains, so we hoped that the roadside eateries we pulled into would provide good food, friendly service, reasonable prices and cleanliness. Howard Johnson's restaurants, with their "famous fried sweet clams" and twenty-eight cream flavors, had not spread to the West. Instead, we often ate at truck stops because, my uncle argued dubiously, "truck drivers always know where the best food is."

To find decent overnight accommodations today we can make reservations in advance on our handheld devices at one of the hotel chains scattered along the interstate highways.

In 1962, however, with more than ninety percent of the motels being independently owned, travelers rarely booked in advance. Instead, they drove as far as they could in hopes of finding a decent motel that did not display a blinking "no vacancy" message.

Motels lured guests with spectacular neon signs touting such luxuries as color TV, air-conditioning and a swimming pool. They often bore the owner's name, and no two were alike. Most served their purpose well, but many did not. Motels, short for motor hotels, were started in California in the 1920s, and by the time I traveled west in 1962, there were some 60,000 nationwide. The industry, however, was undergoing a major transformation.

In 1951, Memphis businessman Kemmons Wilson took his family on a vacation, spending the night at several motels that were grossly inadequate. He later said, "I then realized how many families there were taking vacations and how they needed a nice place to stay every night."

Returning to Memphis, he developed a different motel concept. Every room would have air-conditioning, a television and a telephone. His motels would feature swimming pools, vending machines, free ice -- and children could stay in their parents' room free.

Borrowing the name from a popular Bing Crosby movie, Wilson called his new motels Holiday Inns. He set a goal of building four hundred nationwide, all alike, all within a day's drive of one another. By the early 1970s, he had far exceeded his original vision when he opened his one-thousandth Holiday Inn. It, like most he built, was located near a busy exit on the rapidly developing interstate highway system.

Featured on the cover of Time magazine in 1972, Wilson was hailed for transforming the motel "from the old wayside flea-bag into the most popular home away from home."

In time, most idiosyncratic, independently owned motels were supplanted by chain "hotels" that are virtually the same everywhere. As Wilson argued, the cookie-cutter approach meant that travelers knew what they were getting in advance.

The same held true with roadside chain restaurants that began to cluster near the chain motels in the late 1970s. In Wilson's opinion, the best surprise for travelers was no surprise.

My trip west in 1962 was far different from the early challenges our ancestors faced in their covered wagons, but it still was an adventure. It definitely lacked the bland sameness that marks long-distance travel today.

Would I be willing to go back to those "good old days" of travel? No, but I do miss having a scrumptious breakfast like the ones served at Raines Motel in Valentine, Nebraska, in 1962, rather than the microwaved omelets I eat with plastic utensils on Styrofoam plates at almost any one of the nation's cookie-cutter hotels.

Richmond Times Dispatch, January 19, 2014

PART VI

HEROES
AND VILLAINS
AND
PEOPLE WHO MADE
A DIFFERENCE

Can individuals affect the course of history? Most of us would agree that they can. It would be hard to argue that the past would have been the same had there been no Caesar, Jesus, Mohammed, George Washington, Napoleon, Karl Marx, or Hitler.

The following essays reflect on a few people who helped shape the future. They did not know it then, but we have the advantage of looking at them from a different perspective—in hindsight. We know that in one way or another that their deeds on the battlefield, written words, or actions in defiance of others made a difference in their time and, in a number of cases, our time.

51

GEORGE WASHINGTON: AMERICA'S FIRST GREAT GENERAL

Walk the grounds of the United States Military Academy at West Point and you will see reminders of the great captains this remarkable school has produced. Statues of Eisenhower, MacArthur, and Patton are there to inspire cadets to become great leaders. One statue, however, dominates the others. Standing in front of the huge dining hall and barracks complex is a large icon of another great general who was not an alumnus or a professional soldier, and who thought of himself more as a farmer than anything else. It is, of course, George Washington.

West Point has it right by giving Washington center stage. He was one of America's greatest generals, and his influence on the future of this country's military was profound. You will be hard pressed to find anyone else as well suited to lead the first American war effort.

Until recent years, mostly citizen soldiers, not professionals, have fought in America's wars. Few Americans have been eager to go to war or to accept the discipline of serving in the military. Once in combat, however, they have been as courageous and effective as the soldiers of any nation. Yet Americans have anxiously returned to their civilian roles as soon as hostilities ended.

The best American commanders quickly learned what it takes to lead an army of citizen soldiers. George Washington was one of the best at it. What made him so good at the task?

First, by the time of the American Revolution, he was surprisingly well trained and experienced in the art of war. He had no formal military education, but from a young age, was a voracious reader of things military. He made abstracts of Caesar's commentaries, and carefully studied the campaigns of the Duke of Marlborough.

As for experience, Washington learned the trade of the soldier in a practical, but effective way. His early work as a surveyor gave him an understanding of the lay of the land and helped make him adept at using the terrain to his advantage. Although not trained in topographical engineering like many of his British opponents, he knew how to read maps and to anticipate the topography.

Washington also was no novice when it came to war. Serving in the French and Indian War, he learned how to train raw recruits, and how to lead regular soldiers, militia, and Indians in battle. As colonel in the Virginia militia, he fought side by side with the British, and gained an appreciation for what made their army so good--strict discipline, expertly drilled, and superbly armed and equipped. He knew that those traits would be required of the new American army if it were to have a chance on the battlefield.

Indeed, another key to his success was his understanding that victory is achieved by more than winning on the battlefield. Having skillfully managed labor forces (both slave and free) on his Virginia estates, he knew that he had to take care of his troops, and to provide them with food, clothing, arms, and money. To the ordinary soldier, he was stern and awe-inspiring, but he attended to their wants. He shared their dangers and discomforts. As a result, despite having limited resources, Washington was able to keep his army in a state of readiness throughout the war and to use it sparingly.

He also paid attention to his superiors and allies. Because he understood the politics of war, he spent much of his time communicating with state governors, members of Congress, and with French naval and army leaders. He learned early on not to allow political problems behind the lines interfere with what he was doing on the front lines.

Finally, like all great generals, he developed a single-minded, but effective, plan of action to achieve victory. Washington never named or wrote down a plan, but he had one and used it. Several years later the famous French military authority, Baron

Henri Jomini, referred to it as the "defensive-offensive." The concept called for an army to stand on defense and allow the enemy to advance. Then, when time and circumstance allowed, strike the invader and, if possible, destroy him.

During the Revolutionary War, Washington lost numerous battles and often was forced to fall back. He would then strike when the British least expected it. As a result, he kept his army intact and a constant threat to his enemy.

Frequently beaten, the Continental Army fought on against long odds because of the powerful example set by their resolute commander. As he and his men continued the fight year after year, they increased the possibility that independence might be achieved. Eventually the British people lost the will to keep going, and America gained its independence.

Ironically this strategy was applied against American forces in the twentieth century. Several years after the Vietnam War, General Vo Nguyen Giap, commander of Communist forces, was asked by an American reporter how he conceived this concept. His face lit up into a subtle smile, and with a twinkle in his eye, he said that it came from none other than George Washington. It is little wonder that some experts have referred to the Revolutionary War as "Great Britain's Vietnam," and Giap as Vietnam's George Washington.

Richmond Times Dispatch, February 21, 2015

52

BENEDICT ARNOLD
AND THE SACK OF RICHMOND

Ask almost anyone to list the worst villains in American history, and certain names usually appear - John Wilkes Booth, Lee Harvey Oswald, James Earl Ray, Al Capone and, inevitably, Benedict Arnold, who is arguably the most notorious scoundrel of them all. But few people seem to be aware of the role Richmond played in Arnold's infamy.

A brilliant general for the Patriot cause at the beginning of the American Revolution, Arnold gained hero status by helping win a string of crucial victories over the British. Despite being popular with the public, his fellow officers regarded him as a thin-skinned, self-centered glory-seeker. In reality he was something even worse - a traitor.

Four years into the war, Congress reprimanded Arnold on a number of counts, including consorting with Loyalists in Philadelphia and even marrying into a prominent Loyalist family. Stung by these perceived insults and upset that his talents were not fully appreciated, he started passing military secrets on to the British for money. English General Sir Henry Clinton secretly urged him to change sides.

When it was discovered that he was dealing surreptitiously with the enemy, and planning to surrender the garrison at West Point, New York, to the British, American commander George Washington ordered the arrest of Arnold. Forewarned, Arnold fled to New York City in 1780. There the British granted him a brigadier general's commission in the army and ordered him to recruit Loyalists into the Crown's service.

******

By late 1780, the Revolutionary War approached its sixth year. Great Britain's mighty naval and ground forces had tried numerous strategies to subdue their rebellious American colonies. Large-scale offenses in New England, the mid-Atlantic colonies and then the South had failed to defeat the upstart colonials.

Arguing that striking a blow at the infant nation's largest and wealthiest state would be a major setback for the Americans, General Clinton ordered Arnold to take a force of 1,600 American Loyalists, British regulars and German Hessians to invade lightly defended Virginia.

Arnold and his troops anchored off of Hampton Roads on December 30, 1780, and two days later sailed up the James River to seize Richmond, the newly designated capital of Virginia. After ransacking and looting plantations along the way, the invaders landed near Westover plantation, and headed west by road.

When Virginia Governor Thomas Jefferson learned of the approaching enemy force, he called out the state militia, but only 200 responded. He had all military stores and arms moved out of town to the cannon foundry at Westham.

After firing a ragged volley at the approaching enemy, Jefferson's feeble militia unit panicked and fled the field. Nervously watching these events unfold, the governor left town, not wanting the British to lay claim to such a high-profile public figure.

******

Arnold entered the capital and established headquarters at City Tavern. He dashed off a message to Jefferson demanding that large stores of tobacco and a cache of armaments be turned over to the British. If not, the town would be razed.

The indignant governor flatly refused to give in to Arnold's threat. In response, Arnold ordered that Richmond be torched. His men went on a rampage of destruction, looting, and burning government buildings and homes. A steady wind intensified the flames, which left most of the town destroyed.

Leaving Richmond under a pall of thick smoke, Arnold marched his men to the Westham foundry, which they set aflame.

Finished with their second orgy of destruction, Arnold took his men to Chesterfield, where they went on a final spree of looting and burning.

When Jefferson learned of the destruction, he ordered Virginia militia units under Sampson Mathews to harass Arnold's force. Preferring not to engage the enemy so far inland, Arnold floated his force down the James River and back to Hampton Roads, destroying more property along the way.

Arnold's wanton destruction in Virginia only intensified the hatred Americans had for him. After the war he failed in his attempts to establish businesses in Canada and England. He died as a pauper in London in 1801, shunned by almost everyone.

For years Jefferson faced questions about his leadership abilities and his courage. His enemies accused him of cowardice for deserting Richmond rather than staying to fight Arnold. The old charge of fleeing the field in the face of the enemy dogged Jefferson throughout his run for the presidency in 1800.

The fall of Richmond to Union forces in 1865 is a familiar story to most of us, yet many people do not know that we live in the only American city to hold the dubious distinction of being captured twice by enemy forces and to suffer widespread destruction by fire. Nor do they know that Benedict Arnold gained the reputation as one of America's most notorious villains at the expense of Richmond.

Richmond Times Dispatch, October 26, 2014

53

"MR. MADISON'S WAR"

WAR OF 1812

War can determine the success or failure of an American presidency. Abraham Lincoln and Franklin Roosevelt achieved greatness largely because of their strong performances as Commander-in-Chief. On the other hand, Lyndon Johnson's presidency ended on a sour note because of a seemingly hopeless conflict in Vietnam.

It will take the longer perspective of time to determine how the Iraq and Afghanistan wars have affected the George W. Bush and Barack Obama presidencies.

This year marks the two-hundredth anniversary of the first American presidency faced with sustained armed conflict -- the War of 1812. Leading the nation was James Madison, father of the United States Constitution, which designated the civilian president as Commander-in-Chief of all American armed forces. One cannot ignore the situation's irony.

Like other Founding Fathers, Madison was suspicious of standing militaries. In the Constitutional Convention of 1787, he warned that during times of war, too much power can be granted to a nation's executive. "A standing military force with an overgrown executive will not be a safe companion to liberty," he argued.

Madison faced enormous problems when he came into office in 1809. Great Britain and France, two mighty powers locked in war, routinely interfered with American merchant trade on the seas. The Royal Navy, desperate to man its ships, regularly seized sailors from American vessels and "impressed" them into British service. Many Americans were convinced that England was behind frequent Indian uprisings on the southern and western frontiers.

Facing continued British interference on the high seas, and with a steady drumbeat of calls for action from so-called "War Hawks" in Congress, President Madison asked for a declaration of war in June of 1812. The infant nation found itself unready for what lay ahead. Its small army and navy and tiny war department were now arrayed against the strongest military force on earth.

The war did not go well for the United States. Its land forces lost most of their battles; an American invasion of Canada ended in near disaster; and the New England states threatened secession in protest of federal policy. One of the few bright spots was the infant United States Navy, which at times outfought and stymied the mighty Royal Navy.

How did our first wartime president perform? From the beginning, his political opponents portrayed Madison as a timorous pacifist dragged into the conflict by the War Hawks. Calling it "Mr. Madison's War," they constantly attacked his war policies, to which he responded ineffectively.

As Commander-in-Chief, he was hindered by the refusal of Congress to carry through with his requests for strengthening the Navy and Army. Having never served in the military, his greatest fault was in selecting incompetent subordinates.

He made poor choices in his Army commanders by often relying on aging Revolutionary War veterans. Madison was saddled with a divided Cabinet. His Secretary of War was not only unsuited for the post, he often ignored the president's directives.

Neither Madison nor his assistants developed a grand strategy to effectively stop the British. Unlike Lincoln and Roosevelt, who expanded the powers of the presidency to more effectively prosecute their war efforts, Madison for the most part held true to his belief that a strong executive, even in times of war, was a threat to the people.

He suffered the ultimate humiliation when British troops marched on Washington in August 1814, forcing him and his government to flee, followed by widespread destruction of the national capital. Many Americans thought the war was lost.

On the contrary, weary and stretched financially from almost continuous conflict with France, the British agreed to negotiate an end to the war four months later. Before word of the peace treaty reached America, Andrew Jackson won a stunning victory over a superior British force at New Orleans, thus ending the controversial war on a positive note for the United States.

In reality, the nation was fortunate to escape without losing or making major concessions to the British. The war's conduct was hampered by bungling and mismanagement, for which Madison must share part of the blame. The office of the presidency, like the relatively new republic, was still in its infancy -- and occupied by a man who was reluctant expand its powers.

The war produced its share of heroes, some of whom would become presidents or vice presidents, including Jackson and Virginian William Henry Harrison. James Madison was not among them. Usually ranked by historians as an average president, he was the first, but not the last, American chief executive to be judged harshly by how he led his nation at war.

Richmond Times Dispatch, April 1, 2012

54

VICTORY AT NEW ORLEANS
AND THE RISE OF ANDREW JACKSON

This week marks the 200th anniversary of one of the most important armed clashes in American history—the Battle of New Orleans. It was the culminating event of a war the United States easily could have lost.

Named the War of 1812, it started over grievances perpetrated by Great Britain. Interference with American shipping and the impressment of sailors from its vessels by the British Navy riled the citizens of the new nation. Equally disturbing was a series of Indian uprisings on the American frontier, for which settlers blamed British agents.

With growing pressure for action, Congress declared war in June 1812. The young country was ill-prepared for the conflict ahead. Its small army and navy were now facing the strongest nation on earth.

The war did not go well for the United States. Even though the American Navy performed well against the mighty Royal Navy, United States ground forces lost most of their battles. Attempts to invade Canada and annex land north of the United States border failed miserably. The New England states opposed the war and threatened to secede.

In August 1814, British naval and army elements sailed up the Chesapeake Bay and Potomac River to Washington, where they forced President James Madison and his government to flee. British troops then went on a rampage of destruction of the national capital.

Many Americans thought the war was lost. No one could imagine that within a few months the conflict would conclude with a stunning victory and the making of the greatest military hero since George Washington.

Having successfully attacked Washington, British strategists next decided to capture New Orleans, vital center for American commerce in the west. In November 1814, the British dispatched a formidable armada to take the city. The fleet carried seasoned veterans of the Napoleonic wars in Europe, who were ably commanded by Major General Sir Edward Pakenham.

The only force the Americans had to oppose these crack troops was a small army under General Andrew Jackson of Tennessee who had been engaged in suppressing Indian uprisings in present-day Alabama. When word reached Jackson of the impending threat to New Orleans, he moved his army quickly to the threatened city.

Within days he transformed New Orleans into an armed camp. Despite being gravely ill, Jackson worked day and night to prepare for the enemy's arrival. He ordered his men to set up batteries of naval cannon behind defensive emplacements made of cotton bales. He issued a public appeal for firearms and men to supplement his meager force.

By late December, Jackson learned that the British had overwhelmed a small squadron of American gunboats at the mouth of the Mississippi River and were headed upstream. With characteristic energy he declared martial law and assembled his polyglot force—mostly Tennessee and Kentucky militia, stiffened by a few United States regular troops, sailors, free blacks, smugglers and pirates under Jean Lafitte.

The American commander did not wait to take the initiative and startled the approaching British force with a furious attack. Although the British repulsed the Americans, they were surprised by the spunk of the enemy's rag tag army. After several days of probing the American lines, General Packenham decided to launch an all out attack.

Just after dawn of January 8, 1815, a rocket screamed up through thick fog from British lines, signaling attack. Soon a breeze opened ragged patches in the fog revealing the glint of muskets and bayonets carried by an entire field of soldiers uniformed in red tunics with white appointments. They advanced briskly to the thunderous beat of drums.

Behind their frost-covered earthworks, Jackson's men peered into the mist, tense but steady, patiently waiting for the British to come within range. Finally the order "Fire!" was bellowed up and down the American line. The flashes of American muskets and booming cannon lit up the fog.

Gaping holes appeared in the ranks of the advancing infantry. One eyewitness reported that the men in red fell like "blades of grass beneath a scythe." Soon even General Packenham went down with a mortal wound.

His second-in-command then ordered his battle hardened Highland regiment forward, amid the sounds of beating drums and skirling bagpipes. Even these rugged warriors failed to withstand the withering fire coming from the American lines. Within a few minutes their attack collapsed.

The British hung around defiantly for several days, but finally decided to withdraw. Their 2,036 battle casualties compared to only twenty-one American losses constituted one of the most devastating defeats in the history of the British Army.

The irony of it all was that those deaths were unnecessary. With news traveling slowly then, neither side knew that 15 days earlier the United States and Great Britain had signed a peace treaty in Belgium.

Had it been an avoidable war? Probably. Was it significant? Absolutely. For the American people, their young and still fragile nation had once again defeated the powerful British. Particularly after New Orleans they believed that they, too, were becoming a great nation.

Even more significant was the emergence of Andrew Jackson as a genuine hero. His astonishing victory over some of world's best soldiers eventually led him to a two-term presidency, which he transformed into a much more powerful office than anyone before him. Those terrible hours at New Orleans bequeathed a degree of fame on him that few people experience. From then on the United States would never be the same.

Richmond Times Dispatch, January 3, 2015

55

THE MAN WHO TAUGHT
AMERICA TO READ:
WILLIAM HOLMES MCGUFFEY

Over the years I have been surprised by University of Virginia alumni who do not know who William Holmes McGuffey was. Occasionally they will mention McGuffey Hall without realizing that its namesake was one of the most distinguished faculty members in the university's history. He was also one of American public education's most influential people, someone who transformed the way children were taught and how their character was shaped.

McGuffey played a vital role in turning a dream of the Founding Fathers into reality -- the making of a literate citizenry. Indeed, by the mid-nineteenth century, with the exception of the slave population, Americans were some of the world's most literate people, thanks in part to McGuffey.

Born in Pennsylvania in 1800, and raised in Ohio, McGuffey learned to read and write from his mother. He was taught Greek and Hebrew by a local clergyman. A quick learner, he became an itinerant teacher at age fourteen in one-room school houses, teaching children ranging in ages from six to their late teens. He then returned to Pennsylvania to obtain a classical education at Washington College, and from there he was appointed a professor of languages at Miami University in Ohio.

William Holmes McGuffey

After extensive study, McGuffey was ordained a Presbyterian minister. His primary calling, however, was not in the pulpit, but in the classroom. He was appointed president of Cincinnati College in 1836, where he played a prominent role in promoting public education in Ohio. Three years later he was named president of Ohio University.

In both jobs, McGuffey lectured regularly on moral and biblical subjects, but he became obsessed with improving the standards for teaching young people, especially how they learned to read and write.

His message gained the attention of a Cincinnati book publisher who urged him to put his teaching concepts in print. McGuffey agreed and issued the first of his Eclectic Readers in 1836. During the next several decades, his volumes went into numerous other editions, with eventual sales reaching an estimated 122 million copies.

The books with a blue binding became ubiquitous in schools throughout the country. These basic anthologies of English and American literature represented a vast improvement over the schoolbooks generally available in schools. Each volume was carefully graduated in difficulty.

McGuffey wanted his volumes to improve students' spelling, increase their vocabulary and sharpen public speaking skills. In nineteenth century America, elocution was a key component of public occasions and having students do recitations from the readers trained many great American orators.

A man of strong convictions and ideas, McGuffey regarded the interrelationship of religion and education as vital to a healthy society. Therefore, in addition to their strong intellectual content, the *Readers* were characterized by an all-pervading emphasis on morality in which virtue and vice are immediately and materialistically rewarded and punished. The books exerted a profound influence on generations of Americans, and they have been credited with playing an important role in the development of American exceptionalism in the nineteenth century.

McGuffey's widely distributed books made him perhaps America's best known educator. In 1845, the University of Virginia made an important move by inviting him to join its faculty as a professor of moral philosophy. Founded by Thomas Jefferson as the first secular college in the United States, the university raised eyebrows by appointing McGuffey as its first ordained faculty member.

McGuffey came to Charlottesville as a celebrity of sorts because of his Readers, with a reputation for being a vain, manipulative, overly ambitious and often cold man. The move to Virginia, however, seemed to change him. He became known as a great classroom teacher rather than a scholar. His former students remembered him for his keen wit, banter with small children and love of teaching. Over the years, "Old Guff" developed into one of the university's most beloved professors.

Although a Northerner, McGuffey remained in Charlottesville during the dark Civil War years and afterward. Respected for his generosity, the famous educator regularly gave alms to the poor, both white and black. His health began to decline, but he continued to teach until a few weeks before his death in 1873. He was laid to rest in the University of Virginia cemetery, next to his first wife, who had died in 1853.

Long after McGuffey's death, his books continued to educate young Americans. Even today, some teachers use them to strengthen reading skills and cultivate a sense of history in students. They have received widespread use by parents who home-school their children.

How appropriate that one of America's most important educators is associated with one of our nation's greatest universities.

Richmond Times Dispatch, March 17, 2013

56

A. C. Gilbert:

The Man Who Saved Christmas

In 1917, it seemed there would be no new toys under the Christmas tree. The United States had recently declared war on Germany, and President Woodrow Wilson appointed the Council of National Defense to allocate the nation's resources to the fight.

Conservation of essential materials was crucial, so the council placed bans on items it considered nonessential. It did not take long for toys to make the hit list. The metal and cloth that went into them were needed for munitions and armaments.

When word of this pending ban leaked out, A. C. Gilbert, a toy manufacturer of growing fame, sprang into action. He quickly arranged a hearing before the defense council.

Speaking on behalf of his industry, Gilbert proclaimed: "The greatest influence in a boy's life are toys. A boy wants fun, not education. Yet through the unique kind of toys American manufacturers are turning out, he gets both. ... That is why we have given him air rifles from the time he was big enough to hold them. It is because of toys they had in childhood that the American soldiers are the best marksmen on the battlefields of France."

If that was not enough hyperbole, Gilbert went on to declare that toys started a child "on the road to construction and not destruction."

On cue, one of Gilbert's colleagues began handing toys out to the council. Before long, members were playing with toy trucks, boats and airplanes. Moved by what they had heard and seen, the

Alfred Carlton Gilbert

council agreed to place no ban on the manufacture of toys, war or no war.

In reporting the story on its front page, the *Boston Globe* proclaimed Gilbert as the "Man Who Saved Christmas for the Children."

Alfred Carlton Gilbert has been all but forgotten, but if you are in your fifties or older, he may have influenced your life. If you ever played with a Mysto Magic Kit, a Gilbert Chemistry Set, an American Flyer Train or an Erector Set, you know why. Gilbert was responsible for those iconic toys. He also changed American toys from being of poor quality and unrealistic to being sturdy and relevant play things.

Born in Salem, Oregon, in 1884, Gilbert was a gifted multisport athlete who also was fascinated with magic and all things mechanical. He paid his way through Yale by performing at local magic shows. By graduation, he had made enough money to organize the Mysto Magic Company in New Haven.

Sales of his toys were brisk from the beginning, but exploded when Gilbert began publishing a 200-page catalog and opened retail outlets in New York and other cities. A relentless, driven man, he was always looking for ideas for new products.

The inspiration for Erector Sets, for example, developed during his frequent train trips to New York. Looking out his window, he saw steel girders being added to buildings by cranes and other machines. Despite the protests of some of his partners, who thought the company should stay only with magic, Gilbert worked his own magic by releasing the Erector Set in 1913.

Consisting of nuts, bolts, girders, pinions, wheels, axles and miscellaneous other parts needed to build dozens of models, Erector Sets were a phenomenal success from the beginning. Gilbert became the first toy manufacturer to use large-scale advertising in national magazines. Sales reached into the millions, and by 1916, the company took up five blocks.

After World War I, the Gilbert Company continued to grow and expand its products -- crystal radio sets, weather kits and the extraordinarily popular chemistry sets. Gilbert knew that boys and girls loved to do experiments with the various elements, and soon after their release, chemistry set sales rivaled those of Erector Sets.

The Great Depression and World War II temporarily slowed Gilbert sales, but they roared back in the 1950s. By then, the company was the world's largest toy manufacturer, employing some 3,000 workers and garnering millions of dollars in sales. Gilbert retired rich, and turned the business over to his son. He died in 1961 at the age of seventy-six.

The company floundered under the younger Gilbert. Other toy manufacturers started producing toys that were flashier, lower-priced, advertised heavily on TV and made cheaply overseas. The A. C. Gilbert Company closed in 1966.

What was Gilbert's legacy? For one, he showed that toys and play can shape people's futures. A Yale professor wondered why the number of chemistry majors spiked in the 1920s and '30s. A survey of his students revealed that many became turned on to chemistry with their Gilbert Chemistry Sets.

By providing high-quality, realistic toys that imitated the trends of their time, Gilbert introduced a formula for success that continues today.

As for his role in "saving Christmas," it should be noted that Gilbert never was one to ignore a profit. As one writer later observed: "It could be easily said that A. C. Gilbert was 'The Man Who Saved the Toy Industry from Millions of Dollars in Lost Revenue.'" I wonder if Gilbert ever played Monopoly?

Richmond Times Dispatch, December 1, 2013

57

ARMED FORCES INTEGRATED
60 YEARS AGO

His final resting place can be found in Plot A, Row 9, Grave 22 at the American military cemetery near Anzio, twenty miles south of Rome. The inscription on the brilliant white cross reads simply: "Clemenceau M. Givings, Second Lieutenant, Army Air Forces, 100th Fighter Squadron, 332nd Fighter Group, Died 18 March 1944."

One has to look elsewhere for the details of a life cut short by war. Those details include the fact that he was born, raised, and educated in Richmond. He was the only child of a father who worked in the insurance business and a mother who was a school teacher. With America's entry into World War II, he joined the Army Air Corps, became a fighter pilot and was killed in action at age twenty-four when his plane crashed into the ocean at Anzio. He was African-American.

The last fact is important. Lt. Givings was a member of the famed Tuskegee Airmen, a special unit formed in 1942 as part of American armed forces that were as strictly segregated as any community in the deep South. Nearly ten percent of American military personnel in World War II were black, serving in all theaters of the conflict. But theirs was a war in which the specter of Jim Crow policies often relegated them to secondary roles and service in segregated units led by white officers.

A common story was circulated then about a group of black army recruits who stopped at a roadside café in the South. They were told to go to the back door to be served lunch while a group of German POWs was allowed to enter through the front and eat in the main dining room.

That story may be apocryphal, but it is symbolic of a profound paradox. While the United States threw all of its might into a war to defeat Nazi Germany and Imperial Japan, it did so with large numbers of uniformed personnel who were denied the full fruits of American citizenship. Many a black serviceman wondered why he was fighting to save the world for democracy only to return home to a country that seemed less than democratic.

Recently a group of Virginia Historical Society members traveled with me to Italy to study the allied campaign during World War II. Retired Army Gen. Jack Mountcastle gave daily talks on the brutal struggle in the so-called soft underbelly of Europe. During the course of our journey, we learned about how a segregated Army not only represented a flawed American mindset, it was incredibly inefficient and costly. Visiting the grave of Lt. Givings in a cemetery that is not segregated by race provided a poignant reminder of a brave Virginian who died in service of his country despite the inequities that faced him had he returned home. All of that would begin to change within a few years of his death.

This year marks the sixtieth anniversary of President Harry Truman's executive order to integrate the American armed forces. Today men and women of all ethnic and racial backgrounds serve side by side in the military, often in harm's way. African-Americans holding key leadership positions in the military are now the norm. One has served as chairman of the Joint Chiefs of Staff. After this year's presidential election, the next commander-in-chief could be African-American.

The sacrifices of men like Clemenceau Givings and the thousands of other African-Americans who died during World War II paved the way for one of the most important presidential orders of the 20th century sixty years ago. For that, every American can be grateful.

Executive Order 9981

On July 26, 1948, President Truman signed Executive Order 9981, which states, "It is hereby declared to be the policy of the President that there shall be equality of treatment and opportunity for all persons in the armed services without regard to race, color, religion, or national origin." The order also established the President's Committee on Equality of Treatment and Opportunity in the Armed Services.

Richmond Times Dispatch, July 26, 2008

ARMY AIR FORCES

Saturday aftn.

NoTice
↓
302nd Bomb Gp. P.U.
AAB Chatham Field, Ga.

Dear Folks—

For several weeks I had intended on

· SLOPPY · JOE'S · BAR ·

· HAVANA · CUBA ·

anyway.

Tell Dad to apply for additional gas
for my car. Get enough to drive it
to Savannah. I'll manage to get them

58

A Bomber Pilot's Tale:

Harold Leazer

With this year's Memorial Day, I am reminded of a remarkable treasure trove of materials that came in a cardboard box to the Virginia Historical Society early in my tenure there. These things had not belonged to a famous historical figure nor did they seem particularly significant at first glance.

The box contained a wallet, photographs, flight logs, cards, hundreds of letters, and numerous odds and ends that actually helped tell a compelling story of a brave American named Harold Leazer of Remington, Virginia.

The son of a well-digger, Leazer was a good student and star high school football player in the 1930s. He attended Duke University, but then came that fateful day in December 1941 when the Japanese attacked Pearl Harbor.

Like so many in his generation, Leazer couldn't wait to serve. He dropped out of school the following spring with a year of college left. He joined the Army, scored high on his entrance tests and eventually was accepted into the Army Air Force.

During the next thirteen months Harold underwent intensive flight training. From day one, his entire family -- mother and father and two brothers, who were also in service -- exchanged letters frequently. The parents described what was happening at home, while the boys wrote about their lives in the military.

Harold's biweekly letters home vividly described his route to becoming a bomber pilot. By March 1944, he was assigned his first plane, a B-24 Liberator, the war's most widely used bomber plane. Soon, his ten-person crew, which came from throughout the country, was assembled. "All in all, I'm proud of my boys and the way they work," he boasted to his parents.

In late April 1944, he came home for a short leave. Then two weeks later, Harold flew his crew, alongside other B-24s, across the Atlantic, stopping on the way to refuel. After finally arriving at their base in Italy, they soon began flying raids over Germany and Austria.

Harold reported that he needed to complete thirty missions before he could return home. After only five missions, he sent an upbeat letter that nevertheless contained an undercurrent of fear: "Things aren't too bad, but just enough to make us wish we were all back home."

Two weeks later, he reported that his plane had been shot up so badly that he had to ditch it in the Adriatic Sea. Thanks to his skilled landing, he and his entire crew were rescued. The new plane they were assigned soon became riddled with holes from enemy flak.

On June 25, the eve of his fourteenth mission, Leazer wrote a letter that was revealing. "I'll admit that I've had enough of this life," he confessed, "and I'm ready to come home. ... This conflict is so uncalled for and no one wants it."

Leazer's parents anxiously awaited Harold's letters, but after his June 25 message arrived, nothing came for nearly two weeks. They began to worry.

In mid-July, the doorbell rang. A sad-faced old man handed them a telegram. With trembling hands, Mr. Leazer read the War Department message that his son had been declared missing in action after his plane was shot down by German fighters over Austria. Four men were seen parachuting from the plane as it plunged to earth in flames. Was Harold one of them? No one knew.

Supplied with names and addresses by the War Department, the parents of the crew started writing one other.

"Please do not give up hope. . . .I feel sure that all is well with the boys," one father wrote.

Hugh Leazer, Harold's brother, tried to comfort his parents by speculating, "He's alright [sic] I'm sure. . . .I bet we might even be eating supper some night and he will walk in just like a bad penny."

Sadly, Hugh's wish never came true. On September 24, 1944, the dreaded telegram arrived, announcing Harold's death, a heroic one. By maintaining control of the severely damaged plane just long enough, he had allowed the lucky four to escape.

Harold's remains were returned to Virginia soil near Remington after the war. He would eventually be joined by his parents, who never got over the death of their beloved son. Their heartbreak was shared by millions of other parents across the globe.

Amid all of the Memorial Day picnics and retail sales, let us not forget the Harold Leazers who paid the ultimate price of freedom for our country, and those men and women who are in harm's way today.

Richmond Times Dispatch, May 26, 2013

59

DEMAGOGUES: HAVE YOU NO
SENSE OF DECENCY?

T he word "demagogue" traces its origins to the Greek language. It usually has been applied to people who are frustrated for various reasons. This pejorative term has been applied to a host of figures throughout history—Caesar, Napoleon, Mussolini, Hitler to mention a few. Venezuela's Hugo Chavez was the modern personification of a demagogue.

With the advent of modern communications, demagoguery reached unprecedented levels of influence. Hitler and Mussolini used the newly invented radio to spread their messages of fear and hate to people in numbers that would have been unthinkable in earlier times. Radio and later television became powerful tools in the hands of two twentieth century American demagogues—Father Charles Coughlin and Senator Joseph McCarthy.

Dubbed the "Radio Priest" from Detroit, Coughlin expressed an anger tinged isolationist and conspiratorial viewpoint of current events that had strong anti-Semitic undertones and resonated with some 45 million listeners a week in the 1930's. After the U.S. entered World War II, pressure from the federal government and the Catholic Church finally forced his angry voice off of the air.

Republican Senator Joseph McCarthy of Wisconsin, however, is perhaps the most famous twentieth century American associated with demagoguery. In 1950, this little known first term senator leaped onto the national stage by making anticommunism his personal crusade. For four years, McCarthy, a shrewd politician who understood how to stir people's emotions, frightened government officials at the highest levels with charges of communist infiltration in their departments. He staged melodramatic investigations of suspected enemy agents, exercised powerful influence over government appointments, and won a huge following.

When the senator failed to actually find any Soviet agents, he skillfully shifted his attack to the books that his suspects had written, the reforms they had supported, and the people who had associated with them. Violating the customary civil procedures of the Senate, McCarthy impugned the personal integrity of his critics, calling them "gutless" and "Godless."

Little by little, however, opposition to McCarthy grew. When he attacked the upper echelons of the army in 1954, his bullying tactics backfired under the glare of television lights. McCarthy held hearings for thirty-six days that were broadcast live to an estimated twenty million viewers, who for the first time saw him in action. To many in the audience, the senator came across as a bullying, reckless, and dishonest demagogue. In a Gallup opinion poll his once high positives numbers plummeted and his negatives soared.

As the days of the hearing dragged on, more and more Republicans began to see McCarthy as a liability to the party. McCarthy's reputation then suffered a staggering blow in a famous exchange with the army's chief counsel, Joseph Welch. When McCarthy accused one of Welch's young assistants of communist ties with flimsy evidence, Welch responded with an impassioned defense. "Until this moment, Senator, I think I never really gauged your cruelty or your recklessness. . . ." McCarthy tried to resume his tirade, but Welch fought back, responding: "Let us not assassinate this lad further, Senator. You've done enough. Have you no sense of decency, sir, at long last? Have you left no sense of decency?"

When Welch and others finally stood up to this senate bully, McCarthy's support and popularity began to melt away. Even many of his Republican colleagues turned on him. In December 1954, the senate voted to censure McCarthy for his high-handed methods by a vote of 67 to 22, making him one of a handful of senators ever to be punished this way. Already a heavy drinker, McCarthy began to imbibe even more, and died in 1957 at the age of 48.

In reflecting on Joseph McCarthy, it is not a stretch to compare him to someone of our own time, Rush Limbaugh. Like the grandstanding senator sixty years ago, this bully of the air plays on the fears and prejudices of those who respond to his angry message. He, too, has been insensitive to the people he maliciously attacks. He has callously mocked Michael J. Fox for showing the symptoms of Parkinson's disease. And he has applied the term "slut" to a young woman who was testifying at a Congressional hearing.

One is tempted to say: "Mr. Limbaugh, you've done enough. Have you no sense of decency?"

First time publication - 2015

60

AMERICA'S TEN GREATEST
MILITARY COMMANDERS

W hat makes great military leaders? Bravery? Audacity? Determination? Charisma? Is greatness necessarily achieved on the battlefield? What about the organizers of victory who enable commanders in the field to achieve success?

Here are my choices, in chronological order, for the ten greatest American military commanders:

1.   George Washingon

Self-educated in military matters and winner of few outright victories, Washington understood that the key to defeating a superior enemy was by exhausting its will to fight. He avoided contact with his stronger British opponents, but struck boldly when the opportunity arose. As a result, he defeated the mighty legions of Great Britain and gained American independence.

2.   Winfield Scott

One of the most important military leaders of the nineteenth century, Scott's record as a skilled tactician and strategist made him a role model for numerous future Civil War generals. His brilliant Mexico City campaign has few equals in history. The Anaconda Plan he devised in 1861 to strangle the Confederacy was adopted by President Lincoln and led to ultimate Union victory.

3.   Robert E. Lee

Scion of a prominent Virginia family, Lee earned a reputation as a brilliant soldier before the Civil War. Turning down command of all Union forces in 1861, Lee sided with his native state. As commander of the Army of Northern Virginia, he was audacious and managed to hold superior Union forces at bay for nearly four years.

His bold offensive tactics resulted in numerous victories but heavy casualties. Some scholars argue that, had Lee followed Washington's example by avoiding direct contact with the enemy, he too could have eroded its will to fight.

4.   Ulysses S. Grant

This seemingly ordinary man rose from obscurity to become one of America's most extraordinary generals. Theodore Roosevelt noted that Grant "was a master of strategy and tactics, but he was also a master of hard hitting, of continuous hammering which finally broke through even Lee's guard." Grant's formula for victory in war was devastatingly effective: "The art of war is simple enough. Find out where your enemy is. Get at him as soon as you can and as often as you can, and keep moving on." Grant never retreated after a battle, and he accepted the surrender of Robert E. Lee in 1865 to effectively end the Civil War.

5.   Douglas MacArthur

Although his gargantuan ego became his worst enemy, MacArthur was a gifted commander whose name dominated military circles for nearly three decades. A superb strategist, he garnered widespread acclaim leading an infantry division in World War I; developed a winning formula that helped defeat the Japanese in World War II; and executed one of the greatest surprises in modern warfare at Inchon during the Korean War. Yet MacArthur saw himself as infallible and frequently clashed with his superiors. His insubordination forced President Truman to relieve him of command in 1951, ending his remarkable career on a sour note.

6.   George C. Marshall

Winston Churchill proclaimed Marshall "as the architect of Allied victory" in World War II. A VMI graduate, he excelled as a brilliant staff officer in World War I but languished in backwater jobs for years after the war, overshadowed by MacArthur. Finally recognized as a keen judge of talent and for his organizational abilities, Marshall was named Army chief of staff in 1939. When the United States entered World War II, he oversaw the mobilization, training and deployment of the mightiest armed force in history. Although he never was a field commander, many historians rank him as America's best World War II general.

7.   Dwight D. Eisenhower

Like Marshall, Eisenhower never experienced combat, but was a soldier of exceptional ability, serving in a variety of positions in the army, including as MacArthur's chief of staff before World War II. Soon after the U.S. entered the war, Eisenhower was appointed Supreme Allied Commander ahead of many generals his senior. His innate diplomatic skills made him the ideal leader of often-contentious Allied generals. Eisenhower oversaw the largest seaborne invasion in history (D-Day) and then led the Allied forces to victory over a once-mighty German army. He was overwhelmingly elected to two terms as U.S. president, the eighth general to serve in that office.

8.   Chester Nimitz

After graduating from the Naval Academy in Annapolis, Nimitz spent most of his pre-World War II career in submarines, steadily rising in rank. Soon after the Japanese attack on Pearl Harbor in 1941, the mild-mannered Nimitz was named commander of the U.S. Pacific Fleet, which was in shambles and inferior to its Japanese opponents. He had the requisite leadership skills and flexibility, however, to rebuild the American fleet into the mightiest naval force in history. Working more in competition with than in cooperation with MacArthur's western Pacific command, Nimitz played a major role in the ultimate defeat of Japan.

9.   Henry H. "Hap" Arnold

Often overshadowed by more famous World War II luminaries, Arnold's role in the defeat of the Axis was huge. An early military aviator, he was named chief of the Army Air Corps in 1938 and advocated an independent air force. World War II interrupted that effort. Starting the war with only 1,700 planes, many obsolete, Arnold oversaw the Air Corps' expansion to more than 80,000 aircraft, making it the largest air force ever. His mighty air armada was an indispensable factor in defeating the Axis powers throughout the world. His dream for a separate Air Force finally became reality in 1947.

10.   It's your turn.

Who would you put in this tenth slot?

Illustration by Dwayne Carpenter

PART VII

FUNDRAISING

AND THE

NONPROFIT WORLD

Recently I estimated that I have given hundreds of talks on the subject of fundraising. Lately, I have opened my talks by joking, "There's good news, and there's bad news. The good news is that there are more nonprofit institutions in the United States than any other country. Now for the bad news; there are more nonprofit institutions in the United States than in any other country."

As you will see in the following essays, charitable giving and fundraising have become a way of life in America. I spent a good part of my career raising money. Did I enjoy it? For the most part, especially when I was at the Virginia Historical Society. But after wrapping up our third capital campaign, and having raised more than $110 million, the thought of doing another major drive held little appeal to me. The financial pressures facing nonprofits are never ending, and, therefore the pursuit of money is relentless.

61

WHY DO AMERICANS GIVE?

W hen it comes to philanthropy, Americans are remarkably generous. Nearly eighty-five percent of United
States households give to charitable and religious
organizations annually, by far the highest percentage in the world.

No doubt, the ability to receive a tax deduction contributes
to that generosity, a privilege that citizens in most other countries
do not have. But the majority of donors do it for other reasons,
from simply supporting fundraisers for their children's band
booster club to wanting to transform an institution.

After a long slog through a weak economy, nonprofit
organizations of all kinds are preparing to launch capital campaigns throughout the country. The amount of money to be raised
is staggering. I am aware of proposed or ongoing campaigns for
Richmond-area universities and colleges, and scores of other local
nonprofit organizations, approaching $2 billion.

Which of these campaigns will succeed? For the most part
it boils down to matching the interests of donors with an institution's needs. Determining what motivates donors is important as
well. I have concluded that people give for four basic reasons.
They are:

1.   Forced giving

Donors are pressured by others into making gifts rather than initiat-
ing them. They are reactive gifts rather than proactive ones. Forced
giving is seen often in the workplace, where staff members are
pressured into giving to a particular cause.

Guilt can be used as a tactic to make people give (e.g., "If you
don't make a gift, this organization will not survive."). Peer pres-

sure is often associated with forced giving, as in, "We want everyone in this church to give to the building fund. God expects it."

Forced giving may work in the short run, but it rarely results in large gifts or loyal donors. It can create resentment that is difficult to overcome and is a tactic that fundraisers are best to avoid.

2.   Vanity giving

Some people donate in hopes of achieving social status and name recognition. Making a gift can place the donor's name alongside community movers and shakers. Often, vanity gifts are large and come with expectations, such as board membership or some influence in the institution's business.

Vanity gifts can make a huge difference in the success of a large capital campaign, but sometimes they need to be handled with care if strings are attached to them or if the demands for recognition do not conform to an institution's standards and policies.

3.   Duty-bound or obligatory giving

These donors feel a sense of obligation to give to a cause that has had a positive influence in their lives or has helped relieve suffering. This form of giving is sometimes referred to as "payback philanthropy" and is often associated with a donor's support of an alma mater or religious institution.

A family that has experienced a particular disease often feels duty-bound to help seek a cure. This type of giving also is frequently connected to board membership, with trustees understanding that one of their duties is supporting the institution financially.

Duty-bound giving is something that organizations should attempt to inculcate in their supporters and potential donors. Developing an effective program around this concept can give an institution sustained support and a strengthened financial underpinning.

4.   Inspirational giving

This form of giving is the most generous and exciting. Inspirational gifts often are in response to novel initiatives by an existing institution or the establishment of an altogether new organization.

A dynamic CEO or board chairman can play an instrumental role in securing such gifts, having effectively cultivated the donors and then encouraged them to give. But sometimes donors are inspired to contribute on their own, as an outright gift or as a bequest. Such donations may come as a surprise.

An unanticipated $50 million gift from E. Claiborne Robins in 1969 transformed the University of Richmond over time from a good regional college into a nationally competitive university. All fundraising efforts should attempt to inspire potential donors.

A truism of philanthropy is that "people give to people." Indeed, nonprofit institutions with respected fundraising records are usually blessed with strong and dynamic leaders who command respect and have influence. But their success is based on two other significant factors -- the institution's mission and how well it carries out that mission.

Potential donors must believe that the institution is relevant, is serving the public in an effective and meaningful way, and is well-run. With those factors in place, those organizations with a compelling cause can successfully attract donors who are inspired to ensure their success.

Richmond Times Dispatch, July 8, 2012

62

PREPARE FOR THE COMING TSUNAMI
OF FUNDRAISING

These are tough times for nonprofits in America. Heavily dependent on raising money from the private sector, organizations have been finding the dollars harder to come by in recent years.

According to a new report by the Giving USA Foundation, last year charitable donations declined in current dollars for the first time since 1987, a reflection of the country being mired in recession.

This drop has led to significant reductions in programs and services at many nonprofits. Most have had to do as much, if not more, with fewer resources.

Some that struggled during good times are barely holding on and may not survive. Perhaps that is not all bad. Numerous experts argue that the country has too many nonprofits (2.5 million), many with overlapping or competing missions, supported by insufficient dollars.

After hunkering down during the recent recession, nonprofits throughout the country are making plans to mount capital campaigns to help restore their financial underpinnings or launch major projects that had been deferred.

Don't be surprised if within the next year some of your favorite charities come knocking for a campaign contribution or ask you to increase your annual gift. For many donors, this coming tsunami of campaigns will make decisions more difficult given the intense competition.

Most Americans give to multiple charities. We also tend to give more to certain organizations than others. Why? Usually the bigger the gift we make, the less analytical and more emotional the decision is.

When I interviewed one of Richmond's leading philanthropists about why he gives, his answer was telling. "I tend to give to organizations that have made a difference in my life or they are of significant service to the community," he said.

Although most people cannot make gifts of great magnitude, they should keep certain guiding principles in mind before deciding where to contribute. If there are any doubts about the performance or strategic direction of a nonprofit, donors should carefully consider backing off until they know all is well.

The following are some suggested questions that donors should feel free to ask before making a gift:

• What is the organization's mission and how well is it serving the community?

• If it were to go out of business, would it make much difference in the community and would anyone care?

• Does it have a strong, united, and engaged governing board that works effectively as a team with management?

• Does it have a good record of board and management stability?

• How solid are the financial underpinnings of the organization - management of endowment; operating within budget; proven fundraising record; strong financial support from the local community; and no problems with cash flow?

• Does it know where it is going by having in place a well-crafted strategic plan?

• Am I confident that five years from now I will be glad that I made this gift, and that I didn't "throw good money after bad?";

• Does the organization spend no more than ten cents on administrative costs for every dollar it raises?

In addition to asking these questions, donors can check other sources, some of which are online such as Guidestar and

Charity Navigator, to evaluate the financial health of thousands of nonprofits.

Recently the Community Foundation of Richmond announced the opening of giverichmond.guidestar.org, a website that provides an analysis of charities in the Greater Richmond area.

People who are fortunate enough to be able to make charitable gifts expect that they are helping improve the quality of life in their communities. It is an investment well worth making. Like any investment they make, however, donors need to do their homework first. With a seemingly unending number of charities to support, getting the most bang for your buck is important.

In that regard, the ancient words of Aristotle concerning charity are relevant today: "To give away your treasure is an easy matter and in any man's power. But to decide to whom to give it and how large and when, and for what purpose and how, is neither in every man's power nor an easy matter."

Richmond Times Dispatch, December 5, 2010

63

The American Way of Giving

Last year my wife and I kept a running count of the charitable solicitations we received. On average two or three came in the daily mail. Nearly as many came by phone, followed by a growing number via e-mail. We were asked in person a few times.

In all, we received nearly a thousand solicitations, many of which were multiple asks from the same organizations. Even so, I estimate that if we had made gifts to every organization that asked, we could have donated to hundreds of charities.

The large number of solicitations we received is common for middle-class Americans like us. For people of greater means, the volume is even higher. In our case, we gave to fourteen charities last year, making us far from alone in our giving. Despite the bleak economic environment of recent years, eighty-five percent of American households made charitable gifts, if you include churches in the mix. Even people with modest incomes gave in high numbers. No other nation on Earth comes close to matching the American record for charitable giving.

Is generosity part of the American character? French intellectual Alexis de Tocqueville thought so when he visited the United States in 1832. He marveled at the large number of "volunteer associations" that had been formed to meet community needs or perform services normally handled by government in Europe.

Americans, indeed, are a generous people, but studies overwhelmingly suggest that they are not entirely altruistic. Some 90 years after Tocqueville's observation, Congress began passing legislation that led to a unique form of giving - the merging of tax exemption with supporting volunteer associations, which evolved into legally sanctioned nonprofit organizations. Starting in the 1910s, Congress passed laws establishing tax relief for probated estates and then for personal and corporate charitable giving during one's lifetime. As a result, charitable giving increased dramatically.

Unlike other countries where allocation of financial resources is directed largely by central government authority, the American system of giving allows citizens to have a greater degree of choice where to direct their dollars and receive tax relief. While there is no question that Americans are philanthropic, I doubt that charitable giving would be as high if our donations were no longer deductible.

In recent years, many countries that have reduced government spending have studied the American system and have implemented some of its elements. They are finding out the hard way, however, that it has its downside, particularly the scramble for limited financial resources. According to latest estimates, American nonprofits now number about 2.5 million, a figure that keeps growing. For all but a few of these organizations, fundraising is a way of life. The competition for a piece of the funding pie - a pie that has shrunk in recent years - is intense.

As a result, fundraising has become a major component of nonprofit organizations. Fundraising skills are a prerequisite for most nonprofit CEOs. It is not unusual for development departments to be one of the largest and most heavily funded on organizational charts. Top-notch development directors can command high salaries. Mailings and other forms of solicitations often take a sizable chunk out of an organization's operating budget.

This is a relatively new phenomenon. A study of nonprofits reveals that up until a few decades ago, most did not have ongoing development efforts. A museum director who started his career in the 1950s told me that money was tight but constant fundraising simply was not a concern. Another nonprofit veteran of the old school told me that if he had dared suggest the creation of a development department, he would have been rejected flatly by his board. "To most board members and directors, active fundraising smacked of hucksterism," he noted.

In part that attitude was a reflection of funding sources then. From the New Deal until the 1980s, government support of the nonprofit sector was substantial. The Reagan Revolution of the 1980s, however, reversed that practice, eliminating or reducing government backing of many societal functions. Significant reductions in state support of public higher education in Virginia in recent years are a continuation of that trend.

Consequently, hitting up individuals, corporations, and foundations for money has become the name of the game. Even though I was trained to be a professional historian, much of my career was spent raising money, especially during my twenty years at the Virginia Historical Society. I did it out of necessity, but also because I believed strongly in its mission.

With the economy still recovering and little chance of a return of significant government support for an increasing number of nonprofits, fundraising will only intensify in the coming years. As a result, your mailbox will continue to be stuffed with solicitations and your phone will keep ringing during the dinner hour. For better or worse, it has become the American way.

Richmond Times Dispatch, July 4, 2010

BROOKS ROBINSON
Third Base

Baltimore
Orioles

PART VIII

A POTPOURRI

Call me a Jack-of-all-trades, a master of none, but in sharing my observations of history with a wide audience, I have not limited myself to a particular subject or field. Many scholars argue that historians should not venture outside their specialty. To me, that argument only applies when a historian is writing primarily for other scholars.

Sharing history with the general public is different. I am reminded of a celebrated astronomer, the late Carl Sagan, who was determined to make such complex topics as quantum physics, black holes, light years, and the theory of relativity comprehensible to the general public. I became a huge fan of his, and I felt obligated to follow his example with history.

Therefore, like Sagan, I have written on a variety of subjects far outside of the aspect of American history I specialized in graduate school—the American Civil War. It has been fun for me to learn about certain topics and then share my thoughts on them with the general reading public. The following essays are the odds and ends I've written about that do not fit neatly into a particular category.

64

WHY I'M FOR THE BIRDS:
A LOVE STORY
(THE BASEBALL BALTIMORE ORIOLES)

Why do we develop an interest in our youth that can stay with us the rest of our lives? Early exposure or family tradition often plays a role. But occasionally it is an odd pairing of circumstances. Otherwise how do you explain my devotion to the Baltimore Orioles for nearly 60 years?

I grew up in a small Tennessee town 650 miles from Charm City, far from any of its media outlets. I had no relatives in Baltimore. As a matter of fact, I never actually visited the city until the 1980s, when I was nearly 40 years old. No one in my family was particularly interested in sports.

I've thought about it and come to the conclusion that my Oriole loyalty can be traced to Miss Cantrell's fourth-grade class and my simultaneous discovery of baseball cards.

For science class, Miss Cantrell required us to learn about songbirds and to make a report on our favorite one. Most of my classmates chose cardinals, bluebirds or robins. For some reason, however, a bird with brilliant orange plumage capped with black feathers struck my fancy. It was called the Baltimore oriole.

That choice coincided with a growing interest of mine -- baseball cards. These unique collectables had been around since the late 19th-century, but became big business in the 1950s, when competing bubble gum companies, Topps and Bowman, started issuing high-quality cards to entice young people to buy their gum. Boys, and some girls, paid a nickel for a pack of six cards and a slab of gum. Because it felt and tasted like the cards, the gum was usually thrown away.

My friend John Smith started bringing his baseball cards to school, especially ones of his beloved New York Yankees. Another friend, Tommy McGee, collected mostly Los Angeles Dodgers.

New to the game of baseball, I saw that some of their cards were of players on a team named for my favorite songbird. I couldn't resist; so sometime around 1957, I started collecting and became a diehard Baltimore Orioles fan.

While my friends coveted cards featuring Mickey Mantle, Yogi Berra, Gil Hodges, and Duke Snyder, I went after ones of Gene Woodling, Gus Triandos, Stu Miller, Jim Gentile and Milt Pappas, hardly household names now, but all Orioles.

I checked baseball box scores for Orioles games in the newspaper every morning. I loved it when CBS's TV Game of the Week occasionally featured an Orioles game and announcer Dizzy Dean would inform us that Orioles shortstop Luis Aparicio had "slud into third" or that second baseman Marv Breeding "shouldn't hadn't-a swang at that ball."

In that early phase of my Oriole love affair, my team played hard but never was able to best the mighty Yankees or other occasional American League upstarts. World Series games were played in the afternoon then. Many of us would sneak our newly acquired transistor radios into school, plug in the earphone and covertly listen in on the action from Yankee Stadium or Forbes Field during class. I dreamed of the day when the Series would come to Baltimore's Memorial Stadium.

It finally came in 1966 during my second year at VMI. My roommate was a fanatical, if not obnoxious, Los Angeles fan, who proclaimed that my Orioles had no chance against his formidable Dodgers. We bet $5 on the series. Truly one of the great joys of my life came when the Orioles swept L.A. in four games, and I collected on my bet.

With players like Brooks and Frank Robinson, Jim Palmer, Dave McNally, and Boog Powell under the leadership of Manager

Earl Weaver, and run by a topnotch front office, Baltimore was regarded as one of baseball's best franchises. The so-called "Orioles Way," which stressed hard work, solid professionalism and an emphasis on fundamentals, marked the team's glory years. From 1966 to 1983 Baltimore had a remarkable run of success and the best record in baseball, playing in six World Series and winning three.

Since then, however, the glory has faded. The move to Camden Yards and Cal Ripken's amazing streak of consecutive games played were high points, but for the most part, the franchise has struggled.

When the current owner bought the team in 1993, the Orioles Way had been declining. Then it seemed to vanish altogether. The Orioles have not appeared in a single World Series in the past three decades and had 14 consecutive losing seasons from 1998 to 2011.

Despite that dismal record, my loyalty remains firm. I'm not about to jump ship for the Washington Nationals, as many former Orioles fans have. My son acquired my love of the Orioles, but my daughter became an avid Braves fan when Atlanta games were telecast almost every night nationally.

Believe it or not, a factor in our decision to move to Richmond 25 years ago was its close proximity to Baltimore. My wife and I get up to a few games every year, but the Orioles always seem to lose when we go.

I keep hoping the glory days will return. Maybe this season, but probably not. Nevertheless I'll be watching Orioles games most evenings this summer, rooting for the team named for my favorite songbird. Go Birds!

Richmond Times Dispatch, March 9, 2014

65

HOW PIOUS ARE OUR PRESIDENTS?

The intersection of religion and politics has been a hot topic in the current presidential election. The candidates running in the Republican primaries have had to publically affirm their faith.

The two Mormons in that race were forced to defend their veracity as Christians.

Newt Gingrich, whose personal life has come under intense scrutiny, has openly touted his conversion to Catholicism and how it has changed him.

Rick Santorum's strong showing in recent weeks can be attributed in part to his highly public views on faith. He has questioned Barrack Obama's theology. In the 2008 presidential election, then-candidate Obama was put on the defensive because of controversial remarks made by his pastor.

Indeed, polls reveal that most Americans regard a presidential candidate's faith as an important element in his or her fitness for office. One is hard-pressed to find another country outside the Muslim world whose citizens believe religion is such an important qualification for holding its nation's highest post.

What observations can we make regarding the American presidency and religion? With only one exception, no president has come from any faith other than Protestant Christianity.

The failed vice presidential candidacy of Joe Lieberman in 2000 is the closest a Jew has come to the White House. John Kennedy was the only Catholic to serve. No president has been a Mormon.

Americans may say that a candidate's religion is a consideration in their electability, but based on a number of factors such as church membership, partaking in sacraments, and active involvement in church functions, most of our presidents cannot be described as especially pious.

The debate over George Washington's beliefs and practices, for example, has raged for decades. Unlike many of today's politicians, he rarely wrote or spoke openly about his religious views. Although he was baptized in the Anglican Church, and served as a vestryman and as senior warden, some recent biographers contend that he was a theistic rationalist, a hybrid merging of deism and Christianity.

Thomas Jefferson, on the other hand, was more open about religion, to the point that he was attacked for being a nonbeliever. For most of his adult life, he was fascinated with theology, the teachings of the Bible and issues of morality. Yet he rejected the traditional Christian belief in the existence of hell.

Jefferson argued that Jesus was not divine and that the miracles described in the Bible were myth, as was the concept of the Trinity. He went so far as to prepare his own condensed version of the *New Testament*, eliminating anything in the original text that did not meet his test of rational, critical thinking.

Like Washington, Abraham Lincoln's views on religion have been the subject of debate. Lincoln made frequent references to God and quoted the Bible in his public utterances, but he never joined a church, and in the opinion of many scholars he was more deist in his beliefs than orthodox Christian.

Until relatively recently, religion has rarely factored into presidential elections or subsequent presidencies. In 1928, nominal Quaker Herbert Hoover won election in part because his Democratic opponent, Al Smith, was a Catholic.

Jimmy Carter made no attempt to hide his faith and attended church regularly during his presidency. He was able to win the votes of a large number of evangelical Christians in his first election. Many of these same voters, however, deserted him when he ran unsuccessfully for a second term in 1980 against Ronald

Reagan, did not formally join a church until after he left the White House and rarely discussed his religious views openly.

On the other hand, George W. Bush was a daily Bible reader, often noted how Jesus changed his life and publically stated that God inspired him to run for president. He said that he did not make any major policy decisions without divine guidance.

What does this say about the American presidency and religion? There is a certain irony that today a presidential candidate who does not openly share his religious credentials can diminish his or her chances for eventual nomination and election.

Once in office, presidents often invoke God's name in public ceremonies. Almost out of habit, they end their speeches with the ubiquitous "God bless America."

But most presidents have not openly touted their religion. Perhaps that is just as well. Unlike some Muslim countries with governments verging on being theocracies, most Americans are willing to go only so far in mixing religion and politics. History shows us that when political leaders believe they are instruments of God, the results can be anything but good for the people. Just ask the citizens of Iran or people who have lived under Taliban rule.

Richmond Times Dispatch, February 26, 2012

66

TEN BOOKS THAT CHANGED AMERICAN HISTORY

What causes turning points in history? The flow of history often is shaped by the actions of people in positions of power such as government leaders.

Is it possible, however, that some people, seemingly with little power or influence, can shape a nation's future? Can something as humble as a book or pamphlet lead to changes in direction for a country and its citizens? My study of the past convinces me that certain books have indeed helped cause identifiable turning points in American history.

Over the years, I have compiled an extensive list of those influential books, from which I have chosen the ten most important titles. All had either long-term effects on public opinion or behavior, or they informed the thinking and actions of people in positions of authority.

My list is completely subjective, but the books on it have one or more of the following characteristics: All were authored and published in Colonial America or the United States. They were not necessarily best-sellers nor do they all qualify as great literature. Nevertheless, each has a powerful, sometimes volatile, message imbedded in its words. The list includes both fiction and non-fiction.

The latest titles on my list appeared nearly 50 years ago, allowing the test of time to measure their significance.

My top ten are:

1.   Common Sense (1776) by Thomas Paine.

In straightforward but powerful language, this pamphlet called for American independence from Great Britain. With half a million copies in circulation, it helped sway many undecided Colonists to join the Patriot cause.

2.   The Federalist (1787) by Alexander Hamilton, James Madison, and John Jay.

These 85 essays played a crucial role in influencing state officials, especially in Virginia, to abandon the ineffective Articles of Confederation and adopt the United States Constitution, a system of government that has survived for more than two centuries.

3.   The Eclectic Reader (1836) by William Holmes McGuffey.

Professor of moral philosophy at the University of Virginia, McGuffey was deeply interested in education and teaching. He was particularly concerned with the poor quality and inconsistency of textbooks used in American schools. For more than a century, his Readers served as the only standardized literature text in the country, and one that had a uniquely American perspective.

4.   Uncle Tom's Cabin (1852) by Harriet Beecher Stowe.

Considered by many scholars as the most influential book in American history, this compelling story about a slave family stirred the Northern public to sympathize with the enslaved. An overnight best-seller, the novel was translated into 20 languages, but was banned from distribution in the South. Stowe's work is often cited as a factor in dividing the nation and eventually leading to the Civil War.

5.   The Influence of Sea Power on History (1890) by Alfred Thayer Mahan.

This little-known work by the president of the Naval War College influenced the worldwide buildup of seagoing forces prior to World War I. Mahan argued that mighty nations have mighty navies and far-flung strategic outposts.

6.   The Jungle (1906) by Upton Sinclair.

The novel describes in lurid detail the lives of immigrants working in filthy conditions in the Chicago stockyards and meat packing factories. It helped lead to congressional investigations and the passage of the *Meat Inspection Act*, the first significant consumer protection legislation.

7.   Invisible Man (1953) by Ralph Ellison.

Ellison's story of an educated black man describes the contrast between Northern and Southern racism. This groundbreaking novel won the National Book Award and is often regarded as the first widely circulated to tackle head-on the issue of race relations in post World War II America.

8.   Silent Spring (1962) by Rachel Carson.

Carson's bestseller described in elegant prose the devastating effects of chemicals on the natural world. The book led to unprecedented public awareness of the environment and man's impact on it. Carson has been called the Mother of the Environmental Movement.

9.   The Feminine Mystique (1963) by Betty Friedan.

Reading this was an epiphany for many women who felt trapped as housewives. Friedan argued that women are as capable as men to do any kind of work or pursue any career. The book was a bestseller among women and helped inspire a generation of women to change the status quo.

10.   The Conscience of a Conservative (1963) by Barry Goldwater (and ghost written by L. Brent Bozell Jr.).

For many Americans, this work also was an epiphany. Published the year before he ran for the presidency, the Arizonan's book made a strong case for embracing limited government, tight fiscal policies, and a less idealistic foreign policy. It helped push the Republican Party to the right and inspired large numbers of young conservatives, many of whom eventually entered politics. Ronald Reagan cited it as one of the most influential books he ever read. Some scholars argue that it was the opening salvo in the dismantling of Roosevelt's New Deal government.

That is my list as of today, but if I were to write this column next week, the entries would probably change.

My "runner up" list is long, and I find myself frequently moving titles in and out of my top ten.

Which would you choose? With a wide variety of media now capable of changing the course of history, will books continue to have the influence they have had in the past? Somehow I think they will.

As James Russell Lowell wrote more than a century ago: "Books are the quietest and most constant of friends; they are the most accessible and wisest of counselors, and the most patient of teachers." Call me old-fashioned, but I just don't think of television, computers, and other forms of electronic information delivery as being constant friends, wise counselors, or patient teachers.

Richmond Times Dispatch, April 18, 2010

67

STATE CAPITOLS:
AMERICA'S CATHEDRALS OF DEMOCRACY

During a recent business trip to Helena, Montana, I found myself thinking about European cathedrals. Almost every major city in Europe features one of these grand edifices erected to the glory of God. From St. Paul's in London to Notre Dame in Paris and St. Peter's in Rome, these iconic structures are as much tourist attractions as they are places of worship.

The United States has its share of cathedrals, but they have never been considered central to the history and culture of our cities like they are in other parts of the world. Only a handful can be regarded as major tourist attractions. Perhaps the wide diversity of religion in America explains this.

But there is another type of cathedral that is vital to the American experience -state capitols. They are our cathedrals of democracy.

I was reminded of this in Montana. For years, I have made it a habit to visit state capitol buildings in my travels.

I never cease to be amazed at their grandeur and how they often resemble cathedrals, especially in places like Topeka, Pierre, Harrisburg, Indianapolis, and Helena.

Each reflects pride of state in its architecture and design. Each is a cultural and historic treasure.

Of the fifty state capitols, more than half are downsized imitations of the U. S. Capitol, which in turn resembles St. Paul's and St. Peter's cathedrals. The other state capitols differ greatly in form, from very modern buildings in Honolulu and Santa Fe to the Thomas Jefferson-designed structure in Richmond and the antebellum Greek revival Tennessee state capitol, where its architect is entombed in its north wall.

Dover, Delaware, is home of a capitol building that looks as if it comes from right out of the eighteenth century - but it actually dates from the 1930s.

The almost identical capitols of Louisiana and Nebraska combine Classical and Gothic architectural traditions; but look closely at some of their Art Deco features inside and you quickly realize that they were built in the 1930s.

As grand as state capitol buildings are, with the exception of Virginia's and a few others, most cannot be held up as architectural gems. On the other hand, it is often what is found inside these buildings that awes the visitor.

Thirty-five vibrant history murals grace the walls of the Montana statehouse, which also contains grand paintings by prominent artists, including Charles M. Russell.

The architect of Pennsylvania's capitol, Joseph Huston, envisioned it as a "Palace of Art," a dream that became reality. Dedicated in 1906, this centerpiece of downtown Harrisburg features spectacular paintings, stained glass, murals, and furnishings by some of the best artisans of the day.

Kansas pays homage to the only person convicted of treason who is featured in a state capitol - John Steuart Curry's powerful mural portraying abolitionist John Brown.

Visitors to the Missouri capitol will find a series of dramatic murals by Thomas Hart Benton interpreting the state's history.

A huge painting of the 1864 Civil War battle of Winchester by Julian Scott in the statehouse in Montpelier honors Vermont soldiers.

Most of our state capitols are magnificent architectural and artistic treasures, but first and foremost, they are public buildings that belong to the people. They are majestic symbols of history and power, and icons of democracy and freedom. They represent something else as well - a means by which the people are to retain control over their government.

James Madison asserted that the individual states and the national government "are in fact but different agents and trustees of the people, constituted with different powers."

Alexander Hamilton suggested that both levels of government, state and federal, would exercise authority for the benefit of the citizenry "if their rights are invaded by either."

As labeled by political theorists, "dual federalism" holds that the federal and state governments are co-equals, each sovereign.

Many people argue that the federal government has grown beyond the bounds permitted by the express powers stated in the Constitution. That is a debate that has swayed back and forth in the halls of our statehouses since the beginning of our republic.

We are fortunate to have one of those capitol buildings in Richmond. If you haven't seen it since its recent renovation, a trip downtown will be well worth the visit. And if your travels take you to another state capital, you will be well rewarded if you spend some time in its cathedral of democracy.

Richmond Times Dispatch, October 17, 2010

68

CLASH OF EMPIRES IN THE CARIBBEAN

On every island I visited during a recent Caribbean trip, I saw poignant reminders of once-mighty empires and fierce conflict. From the massive El Morro in San Juan to a modest battlement on tiny Bequia, abandoned forts and long-silent cannon serve as symbols of the Caribbean's significance three centuries ago.

Caribbean sugar became a source of vast wealth in Europe, and control of the region's islands required significant civil, naval, and military resources from Great Britain, France, the Netherlands, and Spain - the superpowers of their time. Now a tourism Mecca, the Caribbean once was as strategically significant as the Persian Gulf is today. One of the largest sea battles in history was fought near beaches now crowded with sunbathers.

Those old forts also serve as reminders of the rise and fall of empires. Scholars have long debated the meaning of the term empire, but simply put, they develop when a nation extends its power, wealth, and influence beyond its political borders for an extended time.

The reasons for such expansions vary, but every empire has developed because of real or perceived needs. These include a desire to strengthen its financial base and fuel its economy by acquiring valuable resources like sugar, spices, gold and silver, or oil. Ideology and theology have contributed to imperial expansion when leaders of a nation believe their political philosophy or religious beliefs must spread to others. Some empires have developed to achieve strategic advantage over real and perceived enemies.

Experts debate the existence of an American empire, but since the early twentieth century American power, wealth, and influence have grown to span the globe. When the Soviet Union collapsed, the United States stood alone as the world's greatest empire. Given the tribulations our nation has experienced in recent years, is it possible the American empire is beginning to suffer the fate of other once seemingly invincible powers?

The reasons for the decline of empires are instructive. The causes vary, but they have a few common characteristics. All suffered from over-extension and a resulting inability to maintain their heavy financial burden. Empires are expensive to build and sustain. They require a significant investment of military and civilian assets, often to far-flung outposts. They require huge outlays of capital expenditures to defend and maintain the territories under their influence. They require steady and large amounts of income.

Within a century of reaching the apogee of power, Spain was spending much more than it was receiving in revenue. Unable to reverse this trend, the Spanish empire soon was supplanted by England and France.

Winning and maintaining the hearts and minds of the people within an empire's realm often has led to trouble. National governments that fall within the responsibility of an empire at times were propped up by less than forthright means. For the people living within the empire's domain, this limited control of their own destiny created resentment and sometimes led to rebellion. No better example of this can be found than the creation of the British empire and events leading up to our own Revolution.

The words "no taxation without representation" were a rallying cry for American patriots, but they also provided a serious dilemma for British authority in the late eighteenth century. With the end of the Seven Years War in 1763, Great Britain acquired vast territories, including Canada and several valuable Caribbean islands. The British now held an expansive and expensive empire.

With their own people heavily taxed, Parliament and the Crown shifted some of the financial burden by taxing the North American colonists and tightening controls over their commerce. They did so, however, believing that their American cousins would willingly accept this increased authority because of the benefits they would receive in return. It was a naive assumption, one that has plagued other empires.

Although Britannia ruled supreme for another century, the loss of its American colonies ironically led to the emergence of the empire that eventually supplanted London as the seat of world power.

Since the rise of Spain in the 1500s, no empire has remained supreme for much longer than a century and a half. The burden proved too heavy and the leadership was inadequate to handle the challenges. I sometimes wonder if the burden of American empire, now more than a century old, has become too great.

We proud Americans tend to think that the United States will always remain on top, but those harmless Caribbean forts give me pause. We can only hope that President Obama and other shapers of American policy have the wisdom to avoid the mistakes of earlier empires.

Richmond Times Dispatch, March 1, 2009

69

GALLIPOLI:

A GREAT FOLLY OF WORLD WAR I

On a recent cruise from Athens to Istanbul, the 100th anniversary of World War I was on the minds of our fellow passengers from Australia and New Zealand. While most of our voyage took us to see sites of the ancient world, we visited a haunting place that is a reminder of one of modern history's great follies.

There is no such thing as a "good war," although some wars have prevented or stopped worse calamities. Few historians are willing to give the First World War even that benefit. Fought for complicated reasons that are as baffling now as they were a century ago, not much good came from that conflict.

Blundering, misguided government leaders plunged most of Europe and other nations into a war that took the worst aspects of science and technology, and applied them to killing on a scale unheard of before. It solved little, and it sowed the seeds for an even more costly war two decades later.

At first, outdated battlefield tactics came up against weaponry that resulted in casualties unknown in previous wars. As a result, the opposing armies eventually settled into grinding trench warfare on the Western Front of France and Belgium for three years. Occasional major offensives mounted by both sides resulted in limited gains and massive casualties.

A demonstration of colossal military misjudgment was played out in 1915 some 1,200 miles from the front lines -- on the Gallipoli Peninsula in what is now Turkey but was then part of the Ottoman Empire. First Lord of the Admiralty Winston Churchill believed that a strong naval flotilla could destroy fortifications along the straits of the Dardanelles, thereby opening the way to the conquest of Istanbul, then the capital of the Ottoman Empire, a German ally.

A powerful Allied fleet launched two futile attacks in February against stronger-than-expected fortifications, in waters seeded with mines. After losing three battleships—two British and one French—with heavy loss of lives, the battered flotilla withdrew.

Allied commanders then decided to take out the Ottoman strongholds on the Gallipoli Peninsula by land in late April. The mission was complicated and involved simultaneously landing troops at three locations. The force consisted of British and French colonial soldiers, and a large contingent from the newly formed Australian and New Zealand Army Corps (ANZAC). Opposing them were troops capably led by Gen. Otto von Sanders, a German military adviser, and Mustafa Kemal, the Ottoman commander who later became Mustafa Kemal Atatürk, the founding leader of modern Turkey.

From the beginning, the landings went badly. British troops took heavy casualties as they waded ashore, eventually gaining a small foothold. The ANZAC troops mistakenly landed at the wrong beach, but by sheer luck they greatly outnumbered the Ottomans. The latter, however, were skillfully positioned at the top of steep heights, and as soon as the ANZAC troops hit the beach they were greeted by murderous machine gun and rifle fire, which devastated their ranks. Pinned down for nearly two days, the ANZACs managed to secure a tentative foothold.

French colonial troops fared only slightly better, while determined Turkish counterattacks under the adroit direction of Atatürk stymied the Allied effort along the entire front. Soon, both sides were digging trenches, and the fighting in Turkey began to mirror warfare in France.

As spring turned to summer, soldiers fought in brutal heat. Attacks and counterattacks gained little more than heavy casualties. Bodies lay unburied between the lines and brought a plague of flies that rapidly spread disease throughout the ranks.

The heat diminished in the fall, only to be replaced by record cold weather as the deadly stalemate continued. By December, the Allies realized their effort was going nowhere and began withdrawing their troops, after having suffered nearly 150,000 casualties to nearly 200,000 by the Ottomans.

Gallipoli was a colossal Allied failure, marked by incredible naivety and misjudgment by their leaders. Churchill was demoted, and Prime Minister H.H. Asquith's government collapsed.

For the ANZACs, who had never fought in a major engagement, Gallipoli proved to be a galvanizing experience. Every April 25 is a day of remembrance for their great sacrifice.

As our tour group strolled the beach at ANZAC Cove and the ANZAC cemetery at Lone Pine, I was reminded of my visits to Omaha Beach and the American cemetery above it. I kept wondering what it must have been like. I was moved to tears along with my fellow passengers from Australia and New Zealand.

Twenty years after Gallipoli, ANZAC veterans came to Turkey to dedicate several cemeteries for their fallen comrades. Mustafa Kemal Atatürk, the Ottoman commander at Gallipoli, was asked to comment. Rather than gloat, Atatürk produced one of the most touching eulogies ever written:

"Those heroes who lost their lives here ... are now lying in the soil of a friendly country. Therefore they rest in peace. There is no difference between the (ANZACs) and the (Turks) to us where they lay side by side here in this country of ours. ... You, the mothers, who sent your sons from faraway countries, wipe away your tears; your sons are now lying in our bosom and are in peace, after having lost their lives on this land, they have become our sons as well."

Those noble words on a monument near an ANZAC cemetery moved me. In the end, however, I couldn't help but think of the leaders who in 1914 plunged their nations into such a senseless war. The graves at Gallipoli were ultimately their doing.

70

Twentieth Century Great Britain and the Crushing Burden of Empire

O n a recent trip to England and Wales, I became aware of two signal events next year -- the 100th and 75th anniversaries respectively of the beginnings of World Wars I and II. I was reminded of this by the monuments I saw in almost every village we visited. Even the smallest communities have inscribed the names of dozens of local boys who never returned home from places such as Passchendaele, the Somme, Ypres, Dunkirk, Singapore, El Alamein or Normandy. It seems that little thought is being given to these crucial events in history.

One woman I met told me that, in reality, the wars were a setback for Great Britain. "Churchill said it was our finest hour, but we were never the same. In many ways, it was our saddest hour," she observed.

In 1900, Great Britain was the world's dominant power. The Union Jack spanned the globe, marking the relatively small island nation as the world's largest and most influential empire, encompassing more than ten million square miles of territory and nearly 500 million people. The Royal Navy was the mightiest fighting force on Earth.

Along with power and wealth came a sense of responsibility -- the burden of empire.

Great Britain adopted the role of global policeman. In addition to the formal control it asserted over its own minions, the country's dominant position in world trade greatly influenced the economies of many other nations.

As with many great powers throughout history, however, Great Britain found the cost of empire increasingly onerous, especially during war. When Germany launched a massive invasion of Belgium and France in 1914, Great Britain immediately sided with France and committed everything to the effort for the next four years. Although it emerged victorious, the price was high.

In addition to suffering nearly a million casualties in World War I, the British experienced an economic catastrophe. The country went from being the world's largest overseas investor to being its biggest debtor, with interest payments reaching nearly 40 percent of its national budget.

Inflation soared and, after the Treaty of Versailles, Great Britain found itself in charge of an even larger empire with millions more subjects that had been handed over by the defeated German and Ottoman empires. The onset of a worldwide depression in the 1930s only worsened matters.

In the meantime, the United States seemed to go in the opposite direction. Although it tried to remain neutral in World War I, America eventually joined the Allied side in 1917; its industrial production boomed in response to wartime demand.

Because little preparation had been made for a possible American entry into the conflict, the United States did not effectively enter combat until its last months. Although American troops played a crucial role in Germany's ultimate defeat, it suffered far fewer casualties than those of its allies.

The war marked a turning point in history. It reduced the global influence of Great Britain and other European powers, and it enabled the United States to emerge as a nation to contend with.

Unlike Great Britain, the United States came out of the war as a creditor nation, far wealthier than it was going in. Even though its people suffered terribly during the Great Depression, by the late 1930s, America was poised to restart its powerful economic engine.

In the meantime, Great Britain continued to struggle at home and abroad, as many of its far-flung territories began to advocate for independence. Britain stood by idly when tyrants emerged in Germany and Italy, rebuilt their countries' armed forces and began to gobble up territory in Europe and Africa. When Germany invaded Poland in 1939, Britain found itself at war again after only two decades of peace.

By 1945, the once mighty nation was exhausted in almost every respect. Another 450,000 war deaths added more names to the monuments in village squares. A quarter of Great Britain's treasure was spent. Wartime rationing remained in place for another decade. Highly polarized political factions clashed over whether to sustain or shrink the empire. The country's declining coffers eventually led to a far smaller British footprint in the world.

Spared the physical destruction of war, the United States emerged as the most prosperous nation on Earth, and with a deepened sense of responsibility. A mighty American navy patrolled the seven seas. Americans in uniform fought and died in places named Inchon, Hue, Fallujah and Kandahar. As writer John Dos Passos noted soon after World War II: "We (have) learned that for a people as for a man, the road to greatness is very hard."

Since ancient times, every empire has eventually collapsed under the burden it assumed. One can only wonder how long the United States can carry the load of the world on its back.

Richmond Times Dispatch, August 18, 2013

71

THE APPROACHING EASTERN MEGALOPOLIS

As I gazed out my window on a flight from Boston to Richmond one evening, I saw a vast corridor of lights from Boston to just south of Washington, marking an almost unbroken conglomeration of some 45 million people. This brilliant spectacle reminded me of a term coined by French geographer Jean Gottmann in 1961 -- "Megalopolis."

Derived from Greek, meaning "very large city," Megalopolis, as defined by Gottman, represents the massive concentration of people centered in New York City and spreading north to Boston and south to Washington. It is an interconnected network of urban and suburban areas rather than one giant city. But as another geographer, Wolf Von Eckert, observed, "It is difficult to tell where one city ends and another begins."

When Gottman studied the region in the 1950's, he noted that it "provides the whole of America with so many essential services. ... It is a banking center, governmental center, media center, academic center, and an immigration center." The region is an almost continuous system of "deeply interwoven areas -- politically, economically, and culturally."

The origins of Megalopolis go back to the earliest European colonial settlements along the Atlantic seaboard. A few decades after they gained a foothold, these dispersed communities gradually coalesced into towns and small cities connected to one another by primitive roads and by boat. Over the next two centuries, the region grew slowly, but it took off in the nineteenth century, rapidly evolving into a vast urban strip connected by highways, railroads, boats and, eventually, by planes.

This development was tied directly to the Industrial Revolution, which started in eighteenth-century Europe and gradually spread to North America in the early 1800s, eventually kicking into high gear during the Civil War. Northern industrial might, located mainly in the region that would become Megalopolis, played a key role in the eventual Union victory.

By the turn of the twentieth century, the United States was the world's most productive nation, with its factories churning out vast quantities of manufactured goods. As production grew, the way business was organized changed from small companies to large corporations, where many investors funded the enterprise. The corporation soon became the standard way of organizing what would become known as big business. People with the resources could purchase stock in corporations, their fortunes for better or worse tied closely to how the shares performed.

Megalopolis led the way in this economic transformation and evolved into a concentrated financial market. Wall Street, located in the very heart of Megalopolis, became the center of economic power that extended throughout the rest of the country and beyond. Wilmington and Hartford grew into the nation's insurance centers. Other long-established cities like Boston, Philadelphia and Baltimore turned into centers of financial power and wealth in their own right.

It has been more than 50 years since Gottman introduced the term Megalopolis. The region he described remains important, but it is often referred to now as the "Eastern Megalopolis," as other areas of the country have become megalopolises.

A "Great Lakes Megalopolis," stretching from Pittsburgh to Chicago, is rapidly emerging. Geographers have identified a developing West Coast megalopolis that can be traced from the San Francisco Bay area to San Diego. Another one may be emerging in Florida as the edges of Miami, Orlando, Tampa-St. Petersburg, Jacksonville and numerous satellite communities make it increasingly difficult to determine where one city begins and another ends. In time, Richmond may be regarded as the southern tip of the Eastern Megalopolis, which might eventually connect to Hampton Roads.

The growth of these vast urban landscapes has had a profound effect on the rest of America. Analysis of the 2010 Census reveals that the country's rural population is the lowest in our history. Until a century ago, we had been a nation mostly of farmers, living in wide spaces where the people were dispersed. But more and more people began leaving rural and small-town America for the big city, never to return.

As a result, broad swaths of the country started emptying out, a trend that has accelerated over the decades. Take a drive on some of the back roads of central Virginia, and you will see once-thriving rural villages that are virtual ghost towns. According to a University of Nevada study, "large swaths of the Great Plains and Appalachia, along with other parts of [rural America] could face significant population declines. ... They are caught in a downward spiral."

What does this all mean? Perhaps commentator Andrew Nusca was on to something when he recently observed: "We need to start thinking about population less as city vs. suburb or even state vs. state and more as fluctuating, interdependent zones that cross political and geographical boundaries."

As Megalopolis begins to take the Old Dominion into its realm, we can only wonder what the implications will be.

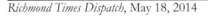

Richmond Times Dispatch, May 18, 2014

72

TEN PLACES EVERY AMERICAN
SHOULD VISIT

I n 1856, the *North American Review* proclaimed that "Americans have a special call to travel and learn about other lands." Indeed, for many Americans, travel abroad has become a way of life. Ironically, it is not unusual to find inveterate world travelers who have seen relatively little of the United States. What if they traveled instead to better understand their own country, especially its history? Where should they go? Recently I randomly polled several people for ideas. To qualify for the list, each choice required one of the following characteristics: It is on American soil; it has historical significance; it is a widely recognized icon; or it is closely tied to our national identity.

From their responses, I compiled a list of nearly fifty places. I then forced myself to subjectively winnow it down to only ten, which follow alphabetically:

1.   Boston

The city's famous Freedom Trail is a treasure trove of early American history. Nearby are sites and symbols of the earliest events of the Revolutionary War: Concord and Lexington, Bunker Hill, and the Old North Church. The famous Boston Tea Party of 1773 gave name to a modern form of protest against a central government perceived as oppressive.

2.   The Gateway Arch in St. Louis

This dramatic icon and park along the Mississippi River tell the story of the mighty river and Westward Expansion in American history based on Thomas Jefferson's vision of extending the United States from "sea to shining sea." The adjacent courthouse was the scene of the legal debate over slavery raised by the famous Dred Scott case.

3.   Gettysburg

This Union victory in the summer of 1863 ended Lee's second and boldest invasion of the North, was a turning point in the Civil War and the conflict's most costly battle. It also provided the setting for one of the great speeches of all time, Lincoln's *Gettysburg Address*.

4.   The Grand Canyon

One of the world's most inspiring natural sites, it almost overwhelms the senses through its immense size and brilliant array of colors and shadows. As explorer John Wesley Powell wrote: "The wonder of the Grand Canyon cannot be adequately represented in symbols of speech, nor by speech itself."

5.   Independence Hall in Philadelphia

The site where the Declaration of Independence and the Constitution were debated and adopted, and the meeting place of the Second Continental Congress during the Revolution and the Constitutional Convention of 1787. Located nearby is the Liberty Bell, one of the most prominent symbols of the fight for independence and freedom.

6.   Little Bighorn

This was the best known engagement of nearly four centuries of conflict between American Indians and whites. Here Sioux and Cheyenne Indians wiped out elements of the 7th U.S. Cavalry under George Custer in Montana during the summer of 1876. Attitudes hardened toward the victorious Indians, and within a few years all native tribes would be subjugated.

7.   Statue of Liberty and Ellis Island

Worldwide, Lady Liberty is one of the most recognizable American symbols. For decades, it was the first glimpse of America for millions of immigrants. From 1892 to 1954, nearby Ellis Island was the administrative gateway for most of these newcomers. Now the restored buildings house a museum of immigration.

8.   Virginia's Historic Quadrangle

Individually, Jamestown, Williamsburg, Yorktown, and Richmond played crucial roles in American history. But within this relatively small area are the sites of the first permanent English settlement and representative self-government in America, an incubator of American independence, the last major engagement of the Revolution, the national capital of the war for Southern independence, and numerous Civil War battles.

9.   Wall Street

The site that best represents American financial and economic power. Over two centuries Wall Street grew into the symbol of a wealthy nation and economic system that developed through trade, capitalism, innovation, and risk-taking. As Gordon Gecko proclaimed in the movie *Wall Street*: "What's worth doing is worth doing for money."

10.   Washington D.C.

This city's large panoply of sites helps explain what America is all about. Visitors have ample opportunity to contemplate presidential legacies, democracy at work, the sacrifices of war veterans, and the country's struggle for freedom and equality. A variety of great museums, the United States Capitol, Supreme Court Building, the White House, and nearby Arlington National Cemetery make Washington a must visit for every American.

****

These suggested places provide only a bare minimum for understanding America, but they are a start. I can't help but agree with English writer Gilbert Chesterton, who observed that "the whole object of travel is not to set foot on foreign land; it is at last to set foot on one's own country as foreign land."

Richmond Times Dispatch, June 6, 2010

73

IMAGINARY HISTORY: AMERICA FLIPPED

History is determined by what actually happened, not by what might have been. We historians are trained to "tell it like it was" and to interpret the past based on solid evidence. We are on shaky ground trying to guess alternative outcomes. History teachers, nevertheless, have long used this device to stimulate critical thinking and lively discussion among their students

Called counter-factual history, it turns real events or circumstances upside down. There are no right or wrong answers, just speculation.

With that in mind, I present a counter-factual scenario for your consideration: What if the geography of the United States had been flipped?

The distinguished geographer Carl O. Sauer used to ask his University of California-Berkeley students that question. In other words, how would history have been different if the land that makes up the United States were reversed? What if the East and West coasts were inverted, along with everything else in-between?

What would a Corps of Discovery, like the Lewis and Clark expedition, coming from Europe have found?

Our explorers would have come ashore to a mild Mediterranean climate, the equivalent of coastal California on the East Coast. As they traveled farther north in this inverted world, they would have shifted to a cool, temperate oceanic climate blessed with plentiful annual rainfall. The only major water route inland would have been in the north, what we know as the Columbia River.

Pushing inland some hundred miles, the pioneers would have run up against several formidable snow-covered mountain chains from north to south that made passage difficult and dangerous. These ranges, known variously as the Olympics, Cascades, Sierras and Rockies, would have slowed the journey and made permanent settlement a challenge.

After our hardy explorers plodded over those great mountain barriers, they would have been challenged by a vast, semi-arid flatland stretching nearly nine hundred miles. At first called the Great American Desert, this treeless landscape was described as unfit for agriculture and considered virtually uninhabitable. Not until the late nineteenth century did agronomists realize that the Great Plains provided perfect soil for growing wheat, leading it to become the breadbasket of America.

Eventually, our explorers would have discovered a mighty river running from north to south that could serve as a natural highway for trade and commerce. Once across what we know as the Mississippi River, the journey westward would have been much easier because of many other rivers flowing in various directions that served as natural highways. As a result, the pace of exploration and settlement would have accelerated.

The good land they would have encountered was conducive to an agrarian-based economy. The majestic mountains they would have come upon, known now as the Appalachians, could be easily traversed.

Finally they would have reached our imaginary west coast where countless bays and inlets provided perfect sites for the development of shipping ports and future cities.

How would this vastly different land have affected history? That was the point that geographer Sauer wanted to make with his students. Geography can shape the course of events. That, in turn, raises other speculative questions.

Would the United States have developed as a nation or as rapidly? Probably not, Sauer argued. Much depended on who established the strongest foothold - Spain, England or France.

No matter who it was, after a relatively quick and easy European settlement of our faux east coast, the great mountain barrier and the expansive Great Plains would have held prospective settlers back for decades, perhaps a century or more. Rather than being settled by people coming overland from the east, chances are that the imaginary west coast would have been claimed and settled by a rival country or countries via sea.

Would slavery have been introduced on a large scale? Much depends on what crops were introduced to the area. If settled by the English, we can imagine that much of the labor force would have consisted of slaves, not unlike the migrant workers used today. Spreading the institution of slavery into other regions of the country, however, would not have been as significant an issue as it was before the Civil War. A slave labor force would not have been economically viable in most of the land immediately west of our imaginary east coast.

Of course, none of this has taken into account the presence of native populations that had lived in this land for millennia.

Had they been included, small and relatively passive tribes would have been first encountered rather than the fearsome Indian nations that European settlers clashed with in the first two centuries of American history. The ultimate demise of the once great tribes probably may have taken longer.

An old TV commercial once proclaimed: "Imagination is a wonderful thing." Let your thoughts run free with this exercise, but remember that none of this ever happened, and the United States is what it is because of factors that are real, not supposition.

Richmond Times Dispatch, December 7, 2014

74

SUCCESS AND GRATITUDE:
LIFE'S TURNING POINTS

The responsibility for success in life has become a hot-button issue in the current presidential election. Republican TV ads accuse President Obama of saying that a person's accomplishments are the result of outside forces, not the initiatives of the individual. Democrats respond that is a misrepresentation of the president's words.

Although this issue has been trivialized for political purposes by both sides, it is one that should not be ignored. It says a lot about who we are as a nation.

New York Times columnist David Brooks addressed it by asking an important question: Should you regard yourself as "the sole author of all your future achievements and the grateful beneficiary of all your past successes?"

For several years, I have posed a similar question to a number of prominent Americans in a personal research project I call "Turning Points."

History is marked by turning points such as Abraham Lincoln's assassination and Pearl Harbor. These events changed the course of history and were the result of the decisions and actions of people, individually or collectively.

People also have turning points, profound decisions they made or something that happened to them after which their lives were not the same.

Through interviews I have conducted, I noted that these people held something in common relating to their turning points.

All cited various individuals who played crucial roles in shaping their lives. Most mentioned certain opportunities that came their way that helped them to become successful.

John Glenn told me about the dynamic high school civics teacher who inspired him to a life of public service, and the senior NASA official who insisted that Glenn not be dropped from the astronaut program because he did not have a college degree.

Former ABC News anchor Charlie Gibson related how his wife persuaded him to follow his dream by taking a low-paying job as a reporter at a Lynchburg television station rather than accept a full scholarship to the University of Michigan law school.

Former Virginia Governor L. Douglas Wilder explained how the G.I. Bill enabled him to finish college and to attend law school, making his future brighter than African-Americans of previous generations.

Ken Burns credits his father-in-law, a psychologist, with inspiring him to pursue a career in filmmaking "in which people long-gone come back alive," and the National Endowment for the Humanities for the funding he needed to get started.

David Brooks observes that when you reach the later stages of life you become "a sociologist, understanding that relationships are more powerful than individuals." You realize that you did not succeed by yourself. Other people helped. Yes, government helped.

I occasionally find myself thinking about what allowed me to succeed in life: the Social Security payments my mother received after my father's premature death; the G.I. Bill that helped me earn a Ph.D. and receive a low-interest loan on my house; the special unit at McGuire VA Medical Center that has enabled me to cope with Parkinson's disease.

I also think about the people who helped form my life: my mother; my grandfather; the uncle and aunt who took me, as a high school student, to far-away places; the college professor who flunked me but became my father-in-law and a dear friend; the VMI upperclassman who forced me to study with him every night so that I would not flunk out; the former professor who persuaded a reluctant me to apply for the directorship of the Virginia Historical Society. My list goes on and on.

I owe them a debt of gratitude that I cannot possibly repay, but at least I can thank them. To those people who are still living, I've started writing letters.

I recently thanked my VMI mentor for saving me from leaving school. We had not communicated in 45 years. I thanked my widowed aunt for taking me to exotic lands. Although I failed to acknowledge the professor who talked me into contending for the Virginia Historical Society job before he died, I did write his widow to let her know what her husband meant to me.

Everyone I wrote appreciated it, and to a person they said they were not aware that what they did for me then helped shape my life. Neither was I.

Now I know. With age comes wisdom, says the old adage. That may or may not be true, but I know that as we grow older and our perspectives broaden, the more we realize that the power of the individual pales in comparison to those greater forces in life shaped for us by others and things bigger than we are.

Richmond Times Dispatch, September 2, 2012

75

WHICH MOVIES WOULD YOU CHOOSE?

Motion pictures have been an American pastime for well over a century. Starting with short films shown in "nickelodeons" at the turn of the twentieth century, the industry grew dramatically and attracted tens of millions of people by the 1920s. This new form of medium altered the entertainment world by reaching the masses. Although films now compete with a vast array of other entertainment options, including at-home movies, nearly two-thirds of the American people saw at least one movie in a theater last year.

I love going to the movies. There is nothing like seeing a film on the big screen with a state-of-the-art sound system. Although I didn't stay up for the entire presentation, watching this year's Academy Awards made me think about my favorite movies.

If someone were to ask you what are your ten favorite films, which ones would you list and why? Here are mine:

1.   *The Wizard of Oz (1939)*

Based on the 1900 novel by L. Frank Baum, this musical fantasy is one of the best known films of all time, and has become a mainstay of American popular culture. It ranks sixth on the American Films Institute's (AFI) top 100 list of best films of the twentieth century. Filmed at first in black and white and switching to Technicolor when Dorothy (Judy Garland) wakes up in the Land of Oz, its special effects were a marvel for the time. Although not a commercial success when it was released, it has stood the test of time and still draws large audiences when annually presented on television. Note that I have not chosen *Gone with the Wind*, which was also released in 1939 and was a huge commercial success. As far as I am concerned, it is as much a fantasy as *The Wizard of Oz,* but unlike *Oz*, it has become an anachronism.

2.   *Double Indemnity (1944)*

Directed by Billy Wilder and featuring actors Fred MacMurray, Barbara Stanwyck and Edward G. Robinson, this classic film's plot revolves around adultery, corruption and murder. Many movie experts credit it with being the prototype of film noir, setting the standard for that genre for years to come. Nominated for seven Academy Awards, but winner of none, this film was ranked 38th on AFI's Top 100 list.

3.   *The Best Years of Our Lives (1946)*

This powerful movie was the brainchild of Hollywood mogul Samuel Goldwyn, who became concerned about the difficulties many World War II veterans had readjusting to civilian life. Also directed by Billy Wilder, the film received seven Academy Awards, including best picture, best director, and best actor (Frederic March). It became the highest grossing film since *Gone with the Wind* and has had one of the highest viewing audiences of all time.

4.   *The Day the Earth Stood Still (1951)*

Released early in the Cold War, this enduring science fiction film warns its viewers that with rapidly growing nuclear weapons arsenals, humans have the ability to destroy the world. Representing an alien culture that has been monitoring Earth from afar, Klaatu (Michael Rennie) and Gort, his giant robot companion, land in Washington, D.C. to deliver a warning to the leaders of all nations. If they are unable to live in peace, Gort would take action and "this Earth of yours will be reduced to a burned out cinder." Bernard Herrman's haunting score is a perfect example of how music can enhance the quality of a film. Herrman is best known for his bone chilling score accompanying the shower scene in *Psycho*.

5.   *Shane (1953)*

Filmed in Technicolor near the Grand Tetons, the story revolves around a mysterious gunslinger named Shane (Alan Ladd), who is befriended by homesteader Joe Starrett and his family. Shane soon finds himself in the middle of a feud between Starrett and a ruthless cattle baron. The gunfight scene matching Shane with bad guy Jack Wilson (Jack Palance) is brilliantly directed, and is one of the

best of any western movie. *Shane* is ranked 45th on the AFI's Top
100 list.

6.   *To Kill a Mockingbird (1962)*

Many experts rate it as one of the greatest films of all time. Based
on Harper Lee's bestselling novel, the story revolves around law-
yer Atticus Finch (Gregory Peck) in Depression era Alabama who
courageously defends a black man on trial for trumped up rape
charges. Finch is forced to expose his children to a small town's
prejudices and outraged passions, and shows them what real courage is. It ranks 25th on the AFI's Top 100 list, and it named Finch
"the greatest movie hero of the twentieth century."

7.   *Lawrence of Arabia (1962)*

Some critics say that *To Kill a Mockingbird* would have won more
than three Academy Awards if it had not been released the same
year as director David Lean's epic drama depicting the experience
of British officer T.E. Lawrence (Peter O'Toole) during World War
I. Nominated for ten Oscars, and winner of seven, it is considered
one of the greatest and most influential films ever made. When
asked about films that most influenced his directing career, Steven
Spielberg named *Lawrence of Arabia* without hesitation.   With
its sweeping panoramic scenes, accompanied by Maurice Jarre's
dramatic musical score, it is easy to see why Spielberg described
this movie as "a miracle."

8.   *Barry Lyndon (1975)*

I cannot think of a film that portrays life in the past better than
this account of the exploits of a fictional eighteenth century Irish
adventurer based on a novel by William Makepeace Thackeray.
Produced and directed by Stanley Kubrick, the film is noted for
its dramatic exterior shots done on location in Ireland, England,
and Germany; its effective use of candle lit interior scenes; a score
based solely on classical music and Irish folk tunes that perfectly
fits every scene; and a compelling storyline well portrayed by its
actors. A modest commercial success when it was released, it is
now regarded as Kubrick's best film. Critic Roger Ebert noted, "it
must be one of the most beautiful films ever made."

9.   *Glory (1989)*

Rarely has the Civil War been accurately portrayed in movies. *Glory* is an exception. It is the story of the 54th Massachusetts Volunteer Infantry, one of the first all-black units to fight in the Civil War. Led by white Colonel Robert Gould Shaw (Matthew Broderick), the regiment faces two enemies – prejudice by whites within the Union army and Confederate forces on the battlefield. The final climatic scene of the unit's attack on Fort Wagner, South Carolina, realistically portrays the ability of African-American troops ability to fight with the best of them. Winner of three Oscars, including best supporting actor for Denzel Washington, the film was an eye opener for most Americans, white and black alike, about the key role blacks played in securing Union victory.

10.   *Waiting for Guffman (1997)*

Combining a documentary with comedy ("mocumentary"), the film portrays a small fictional town in Missouri preparing to celebrate its 150th anniversary. A group of naïve citizens decide to produce a musical based on the town's history titled *Red, White, and Blaine,* led by eccentric director Corky St. Clair (Christopher Guest). Corky convinces the cast that their tableau may eventually make it to Broadway. Having grown up in a small town myself, and having spent nearly thirty years working with local historical societies, I find this to be one of the funniest movies I have ever watched.

That's my list. Which ten movies would you choose?

First time published.

Alethea Bryan and David McCullough at the U.S. Naval Academy, 1994

PART IX

THE NEXT GENERATION

My wife Cammy and I have been blessed with two remarkable children, *their respective spouses, and three grandchildren. I am particularly proud of the fact that three of the four of my children and in-law children, Alethea, Glenn, and Angela, have served their country in uniform, while my son, Charles, worked as a civilian for the Navy.*

Charles overcame debilitating asthma as a child, graduated from VMI with honors with a degree in computer science. To our great fortune, he met and fell in love with Angela Roman, who is now a doctor serving as an officer in the United States Army. Last year, Charles and Angela had a daughter, our first granddaughter, Olivia Edith Bryan.

My daughter, Alethea Bryan Gerding, taught herself to read when she was four years old. She developed a passion for baseball that she has never lost. From her first day of school until she completed her Master's degree, she excelled as a student. She graduated with honors from the United States Naval Academy, and served on active duty in the Navy for seven years, including service aboard a guided missile cruiser and an aircraft carrier. While in the Navy, she met Glenn Gerding, who was serving as a JAG officer stationed in Norfolk. Shortly before they left active duty, they married. For the last ten years, she has served as the managing editor of the Journal of Prosthodontics. She and Glenn live in Chapel Hill, North Carolina, with their two sons, Graham and Jackson.

I knew that she is a highly respected editor in the field of medical science journalism, but I did not realize her special gift as a writer until she sent me the following essay about the horrific tragedy at Sandy Hook School in Connecticut on December 14, 2012. As soon as I read it, I knew that it should be published. I immediately sent it to Todd Culbertson at the Richmond Times-Dispatch, who agreed to publish it a few days later.

Like most of us, I read many articles about the atrocity at Sandy Hook, but none moved me as much as the words of my own daughter.

I am therefore pleased to end this volume with the best essay of the entire lot.

76

HONORING THE EDUCATORS'
'UNFATHOMABLE COURAGE'

By

Alethea Bryan Gerding

Last week as I crossed the Frank Porter Graham Elementary School parking lot, my phone buzzed with a text from my mother. She and my father were visiting the U.S. Marine Corps Museum in Quantico, Virginia. Her text included a picture of a memorial stone for Major Megan McClung. Megan was my classmate at the Naval Academy. She was killed in Iraq, the first female Naval Academy graduate to die in action.

I thank my mom for sending the picture, then ask her to look for another memorial, this one to Major Doug Zembiec, another classmate, the "Lion of Fallujah," so nicknamed for his heroism in that battle. I sign off with "Volunteering in Graham's class today! Gotta go."

As I dutifully check in at the front desk, I think of Megan and Doug and the sacrifices they made. I think of their bravery to choose a dangerous career in a dangerous place. They did not do this blindly. From our earliest days at the Naval Academy, we were told stories of heroism and sacrifice about Medal of Honor winners, men who took bullets for their troops, men who withstood years of torture. It was drilled into us: Don't let your brother (or sister) in arms down, put your troops ahead of yourself, stand brave in the face of fear. That's what Megan and Doug did. That's courage.

I chose to leave active military service after seven years, and only by coincidence did I leave several months before the wars in Afghanistan and Iraq began.

Courtesy of The Richmond Times-Dispatch

As I stroll down the elementary hallway filled with children's art, I say a silent thank you to Megan and Doug. To my classmate Erik Kristensen, a Navy SEAL killed in a helicopter crash in Afghanistan. To classmates Brendan Duffy, Bruce Donald and Rich Pugh, naval aviators killed in crashes at sea. "Thank you, guys," I think, and ponder the choices and fate that led to their ultimate sacrifice and to me being a volunteer mom in an elementary school classroom.

Then I have to stop thinking of them, because I have first-graders to help. I wave to my son and kiss him on the head. I put my boring grown-up coat and boring grown-up bag against the back wall overflowing with much cooler pink puffy coats, cartoon-emblazoned jackets, flowery backpacks with friendship beads on every zipper pull, and backpacks that — if my son's is any indication — contain rocks that I would classify as gravel, but a first-grader would classify as a potential fossil or crystal with magic powers.

I get to work helping the kids with writing workshop. Their task: Write about their favorite day. David is writing about a day of golf with his dad. Emma's choice is a day spent shopping with her mom. Hanna hasn't decided yet but has drawn pretty flowers on her paper. After about 30 minutes, teacher Keri Upson calls them to the carpet to share their stories. First, though, Olivia needs help taking her sweater off. Graham needs to be reprimanded to stop sticking Miss Upson's pointer in Joshua's face. They are almost settled when Alexa is caught braiding someone's hair. Finally, they settle in. Eighteen buzzing, excited, eager first-graders.

The other volunteer mom and I take this opportunity to escape to Miss Upson's small office where we spend the next half-hour stapling and sorting reading material and discussing plans for the holidays. Occasionally we hear someone being reminded to pay attention or keep her hands to herself. More often we hear laughter from the children and encouraging comments from Miss Upson.

Then our time is up. I check my phone. No text from my mother. I wonder if she saw a memorial to Doug. I think again about my fallen classmates.

I'll go back to school again soon, although I suppose I won't be thinking as much about those fallen warriors I admire so much.

That's because for the past few days, my brain has not been responding to its own commands to stop thinking about Sandy Hook Elementary School. I keep thinking about the backpacks and lunchboxes in those classrooms. And when I do, I see a flowery pink backpack with friendship beads like the one I set my bag next to last week. I keep thinking about the math worksheets and writing exercises on those desks. And when I do, I think of David's Favorite Day exercise ("Playing golf with my dad") and Hanna's flowers. I keep wondering if anyone had to be reminded to keep his hands to himself when their school day was normal and hell hadn't descended. And I imagine my own son, Graham, waving his hands in someone's face. I keep imagining the tiny offices and closets where children and teachers huddled in fear. And when I do, I picture the office where last week I so blithely "escaped" with my friend, stapling papers and gossiping about in-laws.

And, God help me, I can't stop imagining what memorial paragraphs would be written about my 6-year-old son in *The Washington Post* or *New York Times* or <u>CNN.com</u>. Would they say he'd just gotten his Cub Scout Bobcat badge? Would they mention that he still sleeps with a stuffed elephant? That he monitors very closely to ensure his little brother doesn't get more Cheez-It's than he does?

I'll go back again soon, but won't be thinking of Megan, Doug, Erik, Bruce, Brendan and Rich, fallen warriors doing a dangerous job in a dangerous time in a dangerous place. I'll be thinking of Dawn Hochsprung and Mary Sherlach as I check in, as mandated for security reasons, at the front desk. I'll be thinking of Vicki Soto and Lauren Rousseau and Anne Marie Murphy and Rachel D'Avino as I walk the hall to my son's class. I'll say a silent prayer for their unfathomable courage and bravery. Women who were never trained in heroism and battlefield glory. Not expected to face enemy fire. Educators doing an important job in an exciting time in a peaceful place. And they did what all those Medal of Honor winners and POW survivors and war heroes at the Naval Academy always told us about: They put those in their charge before themselves and stood brave in the face of fear.

I'll remember these words of Maj. Douglas A. Zembiec, read at his memorial service, "Fight for what you believe in. Keep your word. Live with integrity. Be brave. Believe in something bigger than yourself. Serve your country. Teach. Mentor. Give something back to society. Lead from the front. Conquer your fears. Be a good friend. Be humble and be self-confident. Appreciate your friends and family. Be a leader and not a follower. Be valorous on the field of battle. And take responsibility for your actions. Never forget those who were killed." Words of a warrior, exemplified by educators. May we all do the same.

Richmond Times Dispatch, December 21, 2012

READER REACTION

Over the years, I have received hundreds of email responses to my columns from readers. Reaction varies from one essay to another, both in terms of the number of emails I received to their content. Two columns in particular generated huge responses—"Those Distinctive VMI Types" and "I Once Was Blind." My column on VMI almost went viral as scores of alumni forwarded it to classmates throughout the United States and beyond. But as you will see, not all email responses to the column were positive. The one I chose is from a professor of law who had taught enough VMI graduates to form his own opinion of "the VMI type."

The other column to receive extensive responses was "I Once Was Blind," my account of growing up in the segregated South. Dozens of people shared their own experiences, which were remarkably similar to mine. I regret that I do not have enough space in this volume to present more, but I do include the one negative response I received.

These responses accompany Essay # 23 "I Once Was Blind"

There is a great intellectual and moral danger in retrospective evaluations of yesteryear---especially when couched in such a way as to give the impression of greater perceived wisdom and virtue than people formerly enjoyed or displayed. Examination of the past is certainly a worthwhile endeavor and we can learn much and be instructively guided by a fair dissection thereof. However, one has to guard against self-righteousness and unreasonably faulting the past for lack of current sensibilities. I fear you have fallen into a trap of your own design---particularly in the manner in which you speak about things. Confederate, implicitly suggesting that as somehow unworthy of the respectful attention formerly accorded. Furthermore, there is something sad, even pusillanimous, about using your ancestors as a cat's paw when wearing a hair shirt.

Name withheld

* * * * *

I am 78, raised on Virginia's Eastern Shore, where segregation was still very much the way of life even after most of the rest of the country had come around to viewing African Americans as something other than chattel.

My father was avowed segregationist. There was no doubt that he thought Blacks should stay in their place. To his credit, though, he never once tried to influence how his children viewed the racial situation. He never once used the "n" word. I never saw or heard him speak unkindly of any Black, other than to say to me: "They're all right, in their place." "OK, Dad, just what is their place?" That climaxed a discussion we were having about this exact subject well into the middle of the night. It was only after I called him "narrow minded" about racial matters that the discussion came to an abrupt end. When the locals elected to build a private high school as the reality of integration settled on the Eastern Shore, Dad approved of the idea but he did not have the resources to send his one remaining child at home to the school. (There were four of us siblings – she was the youngest.) I believe he would have tried if he had the money but it was a moot point. In any event, that child, my younger of two sisters, would not have anyhow. One of her best friends in high school was a Black girl. Debbie (sister) saw integration as not only inevitable but welcome. She has never had a prejudiced thought in her life.

The tragedy I see today is that we are not all that far removed from those days in our attitudes about race. We may not still have Jim Crow laws, although the Supreme Court seems to be trying to open the door to such laws again, but discrimination is still very much alive and well. There are still so many who are blind and who will not see. I don't think I will live long enough to see that.

Tom Miles
Heathsville, VA

* * * * *

"I was fortunate in that within the world I inhabited, I did not see from my family or their friends the ugliness of any use of the N-word, nor of the attitudes that would have given life to the word. . . . What I did not see . . . was any African-American my age. I saw adults, but not children and not teenagers. . . . I do not remember, ever, anywhere, seeing an African American my age within Jefferson County, Tennessee. Black students went to Nelson Merry High School, while we went to Jefferson High School, and it never occurred to me to ask why. It never occurred to me to visit that other high school, or to find out who the students were who went there for which I feel a strong sense of shame.

In recent years, I have gotten into the habit, every week or two, of reviewing the obituaries . . . . One day in August of 2012, I was brought up short when I realized I was looking at the obituary of a man who had been born in Jefferson City less than ten days from the date of my birth. . . . A man who went to school in Jefferson City across the same period as me, who worked in Oak Ridge as my father did, who taught Sunday School in his church as I do mine, and who served in the Army as I did. Robert Lewis Wilkerson was his name, and everything I read tells me I would have enjoyed knowing him. I never did know him because our paths did not cross. He was black; I was white, and I once was blind."

Bill Myers
Richmond, Virginia

* * * * *

This response accompanies Essay # 41 "Those Distinctive VMI Types"

Of the nearly eighty columns I have written for the Richmond Times-Dispatch, none has come close to matching the response I received to this one. It truly seemed to strike a responsive chord with VMI alumni. For days I was overwhelmed with email, telephone calls and even a few notes and letters. They were uniformly positive with a few exceptions. The one below from a retired law professor was one of those exceptions. His email prompted a lively exchange between us, which we have kept up. Ironically we have developed a friendship of sorts, even though we've never met. Oh, I should mention that he is a VPI alumnus, who was a high-ranking cadet in the Tech corps.

"I enjoyed your article on VMI, even if it was something of a puff piece. It told admirably of the accomplishments of many of your leading graduates and captured some of the VMI experience . . . . I have taught a dozen or so VMI graduates. Of course, there are exceptions of every generalization, but here are some characteristics I have observed. First, the good ones: loyalty, optimism, and a good work ethic. But then, there also is a reserved skepticism about minorities, a tendency to view women as only housewives and mothers, and downright antipathy toward non-traditional couples. . . . There is also a resistance to recognizing that many issues have more than black and white (right or wrong) answer. . . .I have yet to convince a VMI alumnus to at least open his mind to another point of view."

USING THIS BOOK FOR
YOUR BOOK CLUB

Because each of the essays in this book was written originally as a newspaper commentary piece with a limited word count, none was able to go into great depth on any given subject. Instead I hope that my articles sparked a reader's interest in learning more about a subject.

Although books with short essays do not lend themselves for extended dialogue, I hope that book clubs, library discussion groups, church circles, and educators can use some of my essays to promote lively and engaging discussions.

Below are a baker's dozen questions that can lead to a healthy debate over a variety of subjects. Feel free to make up your own discussion questions.

1.   After reading Section 1, **The Civil War: America Unhinged**, what do you think caused the Civil War—slavery or other factors?

2.   In three essays, the author uses "counterfactual history" to make his point--# 6 "Choosing Sides;" #24 "From War to War;" and #73 "Imaginary History." Discuss how you think things would have turned out if each of the counterfactuals were true.

3.   In the essay "I Once Was Blind," #23, the author relates his experience of growing up in the segregated South, naively unaware of the system of apartheid that existed then. How is your story similar to his or different? What do you think you might be blind to now?

4.   Is there such a thing as "Virginia Exceptionalism?" (see #22) Can you think of any other ways that it manifests itself in addition to the ones pointed out by the author?

5.   A number of essays in this book cover the subject of sickness and health, and death and dying. In that regard, how are we

better off than previous generations? Are there any aspects that were better for people then?

6.   In essay #3, "Hard Choices," which of the two generals had the harder decision to make and why?

7.   In several of the essays (#'s 51, 53, 54, 68, 69, and 70), a consistent theme is the eventual collapse of the British Empire. What were its primary causes? Do you see any similarities to the United States?

8.   In essay #60, readers are asked their opinions on who else should be added to the list of America's Ten Greatest Military Commanders and why? Who would be your choice?

9.   In essay # 66, "Ten Books that Changed History," what, if any, books would you replace on the list, with what, and why?

10.   In Essay #75, "Movies," which ones on the list would you replace with what your choices and why?

11.   After reading essay #39, "Great Teachers," who was your greatest teacher and why? How many of the characteristics listed fit your teacher?

12.   Fundraising is a tough, competitive business. After reading essays #s 61, 62, and 63, what do you think are the most effective ways to raise money?

13.   The last essay, #76, by Alethea Bryan Gerding, about the tragic shooting episode at Sandy Hook Elementary School in Connecticut, moved almost everyone who read it. If your reaction was similar, what in particular struck a responsive chord with you?

NOTES

About the Author

Charles Faulkner Bryan, Jr.

Born and raised in McMinnville, Tennessee, Charles F. Bryan, Jr., is a distinguished military graduate of the Virginia Military Institute. He holds a Master's Degree in history from the University of Georgia and a Ph.D. in history from the University of Tennessee. He served two years active duty as an officer in the U.S. Army.

Dr. Bryan was awarded a one-year post-doctoral fellowship in historical editing to study with the Andrew Jackson Papers, a University of Tennessee project located at The Hermitage in Nashville. He was then asked to remain as assistant editor of the project and edited Jackson's correspondence during the War of 1812, which appeared as part of Volume 2 of the *Papers of Andrew Jackson*.

In 1981, Dr. Bryan was appointed as the first Executive Director of the East Tennessee Historical Society in Knoxville. Five years later, he became Executive Director of the St. Louis Mercantile Library Association, one of the country's richest repositories of the history of the American West, railroading, and river transportation.

In 1988, Dr. Bryan was appointed President and CEO of the Virginia Historical Society. Founded in 1831, the Society is the repository of large and rich collections of books, manuscripts, photographs, artwork, and museum objects that support the study and interpretation of Virginia's history. The Society sponsors conferences, lectures, and exhibitions as part of its mission to promote a broader understanding of Virginia history. During his tenure, Dr. Bryan oversaw campaigns that raised more than $110 million. These efforts resulted in quadrupling the size of the Virginia Historical

Society's headquarters building and a significant expansion of educational programs statewide.

Dr. Bryan has considerable experience as a teacher and has held appointments as adjunct associate professor of history at the University of Missouri-St. Louis and the University of Tennessee. He has published extensively on the management of history museums and the American Civil War. With Nelson Lankford, he edited the best-seller *Eye of the Storm, A Civil War Odyssey*, and a follow-up volume *Images from the Storm*, based on the diary of Union soldier, Robert K. Sneden, published by the Free Press, a division of Simon & Schuster.

He was president of the American Association for State and Local History and serves on the board of the Smithsonian's National Museum of American History. In addition, he served as president of the Independent Research Libraries Association.

He and Cammy, his wife of forty-six years, reside in Richmond. They have two married children and three grandchildren.

INDEX